TURRETTIN

ON THE

ATONEMENT OF CHRIST.

TRANSLATED BY

THE REV. JAMES R. WILLSON, D.D.

A NEW EDITION,

CAREFULLY REVISED BY COLLATION WITH THE LAST EDITION OF THE
LATIN ORIGINAL.

DANIEL IX. 26. יכרח משיח ואין לו

'Ος παρεδοθη διὰ τα παραπτώματα ἡμῶν, και ἠγέρθη
διὰ τὴν δικαιωσιν ἡμῶν.—ROMANS IV. 25.

BAKER BOOK HOUSE
Grand Rapids, Michigan

Paperback edition issued 1978
by Baker Book House Company
from the edition issued in 1859
by the Board of Publication of the
Reformed Protestant Dutch Church

ISBN: 0-8010-8842-9

PHOTOLITHOPRINTED BY CUSHING - MALLOY, INC.
ANN ARBOR, MICHIGAN, UNITED STATES OF AMERICA
1978

PREFACE.

The discussion contained in the following pages is a part of a much larger volume originally published in Philadelphia in the year 1817, with the title:

"A Historical Sketch of Opinions on the Atonement, interspersed with Biographical Notices of the leading Doctors, and Outlines of the Sections of the Church, from the Incarnation of Christ unto the present Time: with Translations from Francis Turrettin on the Atonement. By James R. Willson, A.M."

The volume was dedicated to the Rev. Dr. Alexander McLeod. Its nature is well described in the title. The author traced the varying progress and development of opinion on the atonement, from the beginning of the era down to his own immediate contemporaries. While scrupulously careful to represent all with impartiality, he made no pretence of "dealing gently with errorists." On the contrary, he aimed to "speak out with boldness and candour," and at times even with "severity." His work, extending over so large a field, could of course be nothing more than a comprehensive outline or summary of its subject. After subserving a useful purpose in the conflicts of the former part of this century, it seems to have fallen into comparative oblivion, and has been for many years out of print.

The latter portion of the volume, being the translation which is here reproduced, contained the matter, which is found under *Quæstiones* X.–XIV., in *Locus Decimus Quartus* (De Officio Christi Mediatorio) of the Institutio Theologiæ Elencticæ of Francis Turrettin, with the insertion in one instance of a short extract from another portion of the same work. This part of Dr. Willson's work is apparently as much called for now as it was originally. The various

questions relating to the atonement are still discussed with
frequency and earnestness. The constant faith of the Church
on the subject continues to be firmly held by the general
body of the Reformed; but it is exposed to incessant attacks
in every generation, generally from without, but sometimes
from within, the pale of orthodox communions. And while
contemporary authorship has furnished some admirable pre-
sentations of the common faith on this important point, it is
doubted whether any other work of the same compass presents so clearly and forcibly the truth of God as to the
Nature, Truth, Perfection, Matter, and Extent of the Satisfaction made by the blessed Saviour. The lucid arrangement of topics, compact argumentation, fairness of statement, and constant appeal to the law and the testimony,
leave the careful reader little to desire.

The translation as issued by Dr. Willson was in the main
faithful and accurate. In some cases, however, the learned
divine, by an oversight, failed to express the exact sense of
his author; while in many more the carelessness of the proof-
reader did him great injustice. Pains have been taken to
collate the version line by line with the original, so as to
amend any inaccuracies. Nothing is claimed on the score
of rhetorical finish or the niceties of verbal expression, but
the work as now published is believed to present in simple
and perspicuous English the exact line of thought and argument presented by the great Genevan professor. It only
remains to be added, that while the Board of Publication
approves of the work as a whole, it is not to be considered
responsible for every shade of opinion on minute points, or
every interpretation of quoted Scripture.

At the editor's special request, a pleasing biographical
sketch of Dr. Willson has been furnished by a member of his
family. That of Turrettin is a condensation of an article in
the twentieth volume of the "Princeton Review."

CONTENTS.

CHAPTER III.

THE PERFECTION OF THE ATONEMENT.

CHAPTER IV.

THE MATTER OF THE ATONEMENT.

CHAPTER V.

THE EXTENT OF THE ATONEMENT.

BIOGRAPHICAL SKETCH

OF THE TRANSLATOR,

JAMES R. WILLSON, D.D.

JAMES R. WILLSON was born, April 9th, 1780, in the Forks of Yough—the neck of land lying between the rivers Youghiogeny and Monongahela—about sixteen miles nearly south of Pittsburgh, Pa. His father, Zaccheus Willson, was a ruling elder in the Reformed Presbyterian Church. His mother, Mary McConnell, was connected, before her marriage, with the Associate Church. Their forefathers had emigrated from Rosstrevor, County Down, Ireland, in 1721, making their first settlement in the neighbourhood of Back River, Delaware. Subsequently, they removed to Central Pennsylvania, locating at an early period in the Cove, a fine valley, about a mile and a half wide, lying west of Chambersburg, between the North Mountain and Bear Ridge. In 1769 they crossed the intervening mountains—at that time a very arduous undertaking—and fixed their abode in what was then an unbroken forest, now constituting the townships of Rosstrevor and Elizabeth.

While in the Cove—where they have left their memorial in the name of the leading town, McConnellsburg—some incidents occurred, not void of interest, which have been handed down in the traditions of the family. One of them it may be worth while to record. Situated so near the very outskirts of civilization, the valley was, of course, exposed to the incursions of the Indian tribes, and somewhere about the middle of the last century they actually entered without any warning and ravaged it—burning the dwellings, carrying off the property, and taking the lives also of some of the settlers. At this

*

time, the doctor's grandfather—so the writer thinks—was very aged, almost helpless, decrepit in mind as well as in body, but of ripened and devoted piety. It was in the early part of summer. He dreamed that the Indians had come into the valley. He awoke; slept, and dreamed again as before. He woke; slept, and dreamed the same dream. It was then about daylight. He roused the family and told them what had occurred, and advised them to make the best of their way over the mountain. They demurred, and especially insisted upon the fact that their horses had been turned out, and time—perhaps a day or two—would be required to find them. Just then, the horses came up to the very door. As this seemed to be a providential interposition, the family yielded, and as soon as possible set out. When they had reached the summit of the mountain, they saw, on looking back, their houses in flames. The Indians were in fact wasting the upper part of the valley at the very hour when their aged parent had dreamed the dream that was instrumental—however we may account for it—in saving them.

James was the eldest of a large family. Of course, at that early day, his opportunities for acquiring an education in a rural district were not very favourable. In measure, however, this was made up by the advantages of intercourse with his father, a man of no ordinary intelligence and reading, and with his mother, a woman of robust and masculine mind: both of them being sincerely devout, and living in the fear of God and in the faith of the Gospel. Their house, moreover, was the resort of ministers of various denominations—particularly of those of the same religious connection. Books were not wanting; and what there were, were read and studied with great care. Hence, the mind of the young farmer was stored, long before he began his classical course, with an amount of useful knowledge rarely attained under similar circumstances. He was especially eager for religious information. In his fourteenth year he led in family worship during the absence of his father. And when, as was the case very frequently, groups were gathered on the Sabbath and other days of public worship, or at the meetings of church courts, discussing doctrinal points, James was sure, boy as he was, to make one of the number.

He remained on the farm—labouring, and taking his part in the long journeys over the mountains with horses and pack-saddles, to Chambersburg for family supplies, until he attained his majority. He then entered the grammar-school, established a short time previously in Cannonsburg by Dr. McMillan, out of which soon grew

Jefferson College. Here he remained between four and five years, and was graduated in 1806 with the first honours of his class. He pursued the study of theology, somewhat irregularly—a short time with the late Dr. McLeod, of New York, but mostly at home. In the mean time he married, and took charge, in the year 1809, of the Academy at Bedford, Pa., whence, in 1815, he removed, to continue the same occupation in the city of Philadelphia, where, besides his labours as Principal of a large classical school, and occasionally in preaching, he prepared and published a "History of the Doctrine of the Atonement, with Translations of Turrettin" on the same subject.

In 1817, having received a call to the pastoral charge of the Reformed Presbyterian congregation of Coldenham, Orange County, N. Y., he accepted it, and was ordained in the fall of that year. A portion of his charge which was in Newburg received a considerable share of his attention, and in the course of a few years became a distinct congregation. His pastoral labours were thenceforth restricted to Coldenham. During the years 1822–26 he edited "The Evangelical Witness," a monthly periodical; and also, as before and afterwards, superintended the theological studies of young men. With the exception of three years, during which he was pastor of a congregation of the same denomination in the city of Albany, Dr. Willson remained in Coldenham until 1840, when he was called to be Senior Professor in the Theological Seminary of the church with which he was connected, in Allegheny, Pa.* Here he remained until 1845, when, the location of the Seminary being changed, he removed to Cincinnati, Ohio. He continued to perform the duties of his chair until 1851, when, through debility which had been induced by a "sun-stroke" in the summer of 1846, he became unable longer to attend to them. He survived, preaching occasionally, although with difficulty, until September 29th, 1853, when, his death being hastened by a severe fall, he departed this life, in the sure hope of everlasting rest and peace.

This rapid sketch presents but a faint outline of a life of active and unwearied industry in the discharge of most important duties. His publications—chiefly sermons and essays, besides those already mentioned—were very numerous. He delivered very many public addresses, scientific, literary, and religious. His eloquence was at the

* He had previously been Professor in an Eastern Seminary: in that year the Eastern and Western were united.

service of every call of philanthropy. While he set before him one grand object—the proclamation of Christ's salvation and glory—he ever took a deep interest in every matter of social and public concern. He had an especial delight in the training of candidates for the ministry of reconciliation; and at his decease, a large majority of the ministry of the Reformed Presbyterian Church had received at least a part of their training under his inspection. In the division which took place in 1833, he held the most prominent position in maintaining the earlier views of the Church. His integrity was never questioned. Into every subject to which he directed his attention, he entered with all the ardour of a great mind, impelled by deep and strong feeling. He had every qualification of the orator: capacious intellect; vast attainments in almost every department of human knowledge; a ready and retentive memory; lofty imagination, combined with unsurpassed powers of argument, and copiousness of language and illustration. He was eminently a man of prayer, and in whatever society he was thrown he never shunned to declare the counsel of God. Among Christians he ever urged the duty, and excellence, and efficacy of prayer. His theology was of the old stamp. He gave no countenance to supposed modern improvements. He dwelt much in his ministrations upon the glory of Christ and His claims to supremacy. He was the friend of man, and never faltered in the advocacy of the interests of human liberty.

His physical appearance corresponded with his mental character. His stature, over six feet; his frame well developed, muscular and active; his expanded and lofty forehead; deep-set, dark, and piercing eye; his nose slightly arched; his mouth compressed to a line; his entire aspect marked with the deep lines of thought;—gave indications that could not be mistaken of extraordinary mental power. His voice, not deep, but sonorous and strong, completed the list of his oratorical accomplishments. At his decease he left two sons—both in the ministry—James M. Willson, of Philadelphia, and R. Z. Willson, late of Craftsbury, Vt.; and three daughters, married to ministers of the same ecclesiastical connection. A monument has been erected to his memory, by his friends throughout the Church, and others, in the vicinity of the church in Coldenham where he so long ministered, and where repose his mortal remains.

BIOGRAPHICAL SKETCH

FRANCIS TURRETTIN.

THE family of the TURRETTINS, or TURRETTINI, as it is still written and pronounced in Geneva, is of Italian origin. It belonged to the ancient nobility of Lusca, and appears to have given a number of gonfalonieri and anziani to that republic. One of these gonfalonieri, or chief magistrates, was REGULUS TURRETTINI, who about the year 1547 became the father of FRANCIS, afterwards distinguished as the first Protestant member of the family. For the sake of his new faith, Francis renounced his home and prospects, and became a voluntary exile. After being driven from place to place by adverse fortune, he finally settled in

Geneva, where, in 1627, he received citizenship, and in 1628 was made one of the Sixty. Soon after he died, leaving behind him a large sum for public charities, a blameless reputation, and a number of children, the oldest of whom was the father of our author.

BENEDICT TURRETTINI was born at Zurich, November 9, 1588, and died in March, 1631. He was a celebrated pastor and professor of theology. In 1620 he assisted at the Synod of Ales, of which Peter du Moulin was moderator. He was noted for his piety, his love of union, his resolution, his learning, his gentleness, and his eloquence. Pictet speaks of him as the glory of his church and school. No man of his day was more honoured, but his career was cut short just as he was entering middle life. He had six children, of whom the third in order was

FRANCIS TURRETTINI, the author of the present volume. He was born in 1623, the same year in which Mornay du Plessy, Father Paul, and Pope Gregory XV. died, and in which the great Synod of Charenton was held. From his earliest years young Turrettin gave tokens of genius. When his father found himself dying, he caused Francis, then eight years old, to be brought to his bedside; and said, with faltering lips, "This child is marked with God's seal:" *Hic sigillo Dei obsignatus est.* Francis greatly distinguished himself in his academic course, and seems to have been remarkable for the eagerness with which he attempted diversified branches of study. Upon devoting himself to the study of theology, he enjoyed the advantage of eminent instructors. The most noted of these was John Diodati, another Italian Protestant, who sat in the chair of Calvin and Beza. Diodati, whose biblical labours are well known, was prominent in the Synod of Dort and the Convention of Saumur; at the latter of which he so succeeded in pouring oil on the waters of controversy, that the Queen of France thanked him repeatedly. Another instructor of Turrettin was Theodore Tronchin, also a member of the Synod of Dort and a noble defender of the truth. He lived to a venerable age, and contributed much to the theological celebrity of Geneva. His family, originally from Provence, long continued to be prominent in the little republic, where to this day it has its representatives, one of whom, the excellent Colonel Tronchin, is known far and wide among evangelical Christians. Another celebrated instructor of Turrettin was Frederick Spanheim.

After finishing his curriculum at home, Turrettin went to Leyden, then, and long after, a centre of learning and theology, where he maintained theses in the schools with great *éclat*. In Holland he enjoyed the lectures of such men as Polyander; the saintly Rivet, equally known by his voluminous works and by the record of his death; Salmasius, one of the most learned men of his age, although worsted in his unfortunate controversy with Milton; Heinsius, Trigland, Voet, Hoornbeek, and Golius, the linguist. At Utrecht he became acquainted with that prodigy of her age, Anna Maria Schureman. In 1645 he proceeded to Paris, where he resided under the roof of the immortal Daillé; met with Falcar, Drelincourt, Albertini, and Blondel; and pursued physical and astronomical studies under Gassendi. Next he visited Saumur, the little city on the Loire, famous for its Protestant university. There he heard Placæus, Amyrauld, and Capellus; men whose learning, subtilty, and peculiar views in theology, are fully presented in the *Theses Salmurienses.* He even went as far south as to Montauban, then, as now, the seat of a Protestant university, where Carolus and Garissol were at that time flourishing.

Returning home in 1648, he became a pastor of the church of Geneva, and preacher to the Italian congregation, such a service being required by the great number of refugees from Italy who sought an asylum in Geneva. When he began to preach, such were the flow of his discourse, the solidity of his matter, and the majestic gracefulness of his eloquence, that immense popularity attended him. In 1650, the chair of Philosophy was several times offered to him by the government. After the death of Aaron Morus at Leyden, Turrettin was called to supply his place as pastor. He accepted the invitation, and remained at Leyden about a year; but the Genevese would not endure his absence longer. The venerable

Tronchin having outlived his capacity for public service, Turrettin was called to fill his place. He complied with the call, and assumed the theological chair in 1653. As a public teacher he was faithful and undaunted, daily inflicting severe blows upon Popery, Socinianism, and Arminianism. From the pulpit he thundered against prevailing immoralities, while with many tears he besought sinners to be reconciled to Christ. His eloquence was of the most persuasive and irresistible character. Pictet celebrates his benignity, his pity to the poor, his care of the widow and the orphan, his hospitality, and his edifying discourse.

In the year 1661 he was summoned to a new service. The people of Geneva were unable to bear the expense of fortifying their walls; they therefore appealed for aid to the States-General of Holland, and deputed Turrettin as their commissioner for this purpose. His father had been sent by them on a similar errand forty years before. Passing through Basle, he was received with honour by Wetstein and others of the great men of the uni-

versity there. In Holland he obtained great
distinction, being complimented by the author-
ities with a gold chain and medal. Earnest
but fruitless efforts were made to detain him,
both at Leyden and the Hague. On his way
home, he passed through Paris and Charenton.
At the latter place he first met Claude, and
preached before the vast Protestant assembly
there, of which Pictet speaks with singular
admiration.

After his return he renewed his labours
with redoubled zeal. In the year 1664 he
published against the Papists and in vindication of the Reformed; and two years afterwards, his disquisitions concerning the satisfaction of Christ. In 1674 he published his
sermons, which were received with great applause. In the same year he issued his great
work on Theology, INSTITUTIO THEOLOGIÆ
ELENCTICÆ, from which the contents of the
present volume have been extracted. It is
said that he was very reluctant to give this
work to the press, and finally did so only in
compliance with numerous letters from the
learned in all parts of Reformed Christendom.

In 1687 he published on the necessity of secession from Rome, and on other important points.

In 1669 Turrettin was married to Isabella, daughter of John de Masse, lord of Sauvet, whose ancestors had held the Marquisate of Saluzzo. Four children were the fruit of this union, of whom only one survived, viz., JOHN ALFONSO TURRETTIN, who was born in 1671, and ordained to the ministry about the year 1694. He became a preacher of unusual power, held successively the chairs of Ecclesiastical History and of Theology in Geneva, and was one of the greatest writers of the age upon natural religion and the external defences of Christianity. Inferior to his father in vigour, he was his superior in elegance; and his copious and classical diction gave a charm to his writings, which secured perusal and applause beyond the pale of Calvinistic bodies.

Turrettin's later years were embittered by the distresses of his Reformed brethren in Piedmont and France. In the latter country, in consequence of the revocation of the Edict of Nantes, in 1685, hundreds of churches were demolished, and Protestantism was driven from the kingdom. But for these distresses of a sympathetic soul, he may be said to have had a happy old age, being scarcely ever ill except from a few attacks of acute disease. On the 24th of September, 1687, he was suddenly seized with violent pains. To Professor Pictet he expressed his readiness to die; but said that the severity of his pain did not suffer him to pray as he would, yet he knew in whom he had believed. He repeated many passages of Scripture, among them the words from the 38th Psalm—"*O Lord, rebuke me not in thine anger,*" which he had a few days before expounded to the Italian congregation. Upon his only son he solemnly enjoined four things: the care of the Church, if he ever should be called to it; the love of truth; humility; and charity. To his relative, Dr. Michel Turrettin, Pastor and Professor, he declared his faith and hope, and committed the solemn care of the Church. His charges and exhortations were numerous. His countenance was expressive rather of triumph than of death. When, as his agony increased, some of those who stood by reminded him of his last sermon, on the words, *Let us come boldly to the throne of grace*, he cried, as if impatient, *Eamus, eamus!*   Shortly after he slumbered, and so died without a struggle, at the age of sixty-four years.

It is not necessary to dwell upon the character of Francis Turrettin as a theologian. His adherence to the received doctrine of the Reformed Church is so uniform and strict, that there is no writer who has higher claims as an authority as to what that doctrine is. His distinguishing excellence is perspicuity and discrimination.   His intellect was admirably fitted and trained for perceiving and stating the real principles involved in theological questions; so that he was a remarkable illustration of the maxim, *qui bene distinguit, bene docet*.   To this primary excellence he added an admirable judgment, which is evinced in the characteristic moderation of his opinions, and the general soundness of his arguments.   His method is simple and logical.   Under every head he begins with the *Status Quæstionis*, and, with discriminating accuracy, frees the subject in hand from all adventitious matter, and brings out the precise point to be considered. Then follow his arguments in numerical order, each distinct and in logical succession, in support of the position which he advocates. To this series of arguments succeeds the *Fontes Solutionum*, or answers to objections, which often furnish examples of as pithy and discriminating replies as are anywhere to be met with. There is scarcely a question which American divines have been discussing as discoveries, which the student will not find settled, or at least considered, in the perspicuous pages of Turrettin.

The writer in the *Princeton Review*, (for July, 1848,) from whom the present sketch has been extracted, concludes his article with these sentences, which are well worthy of reproduction here :—" We were once told by Chief Justice Ewing [of New Jersey] that it was the uniform practice of Mr. Justice Washington to read through the whole of Blackstone's Commentaries once a year; and that he did so to give consistency, method, and unity to all the otherwise scattered and heterogeneous acquisitions of the year. We entertain no doubt that a similar practice with regard to the equally logical and more commanding system of Turrettin, would do more for a masculine theology and an energetic pulpit, than cart-loads of religious journals, epitomes from the German, and occasional sermons."

TURRETTIN

ON

THE ATONEMENT.

CHAPTER I.

𝔗𝔥𝔢 𝔑𝔢𝔠𝔢𝔰𝔰𝔦𝔱𝔶 𝔬𝔣 𝔱𝔥𝔢 𝔄𝔱𝔬𝔫𝔢𝔪𝔢𝔫𝔱.

THREE OPINIONS ON THIS SUBJECT.—PRELIMINARY REMARKS:—1. AS
TO THE NATURE OF SIN.—2. THE SATISFACTION REQUIRED.—3. THE
RELATIONS OF GOD TO THE SINNER.—4. THE QUALIFICATIONS OF
THE SUBSTITUTE, AND THE CONDITIONS OF SUBSTITUTION.—ARGUMENTS
TO PROVE THE NECESSITY OF THE ATONEMENT:—I. GOD'S VINDICA-
TORY JUSTICE.—II. THE NATURE OF SIN.—III. THE SANCTION OF
THE LAW.—IV. THE PREACHING OF THE GOSPEL.—V. THE GREAT-
NESS OF GOD'S LOVE.—VI. THE GLORY OF THE DIVINE PERFEC-
TIONS.

THE Priesthood of Christ, according to the Apostle
Paul and the types of the Jewish ritual, is divided
into two parts: the atonement which he made to divine
justice, and his intercession in heaven, (1 John ii. 2.
Heb. ix. 12.) The necessity of such an atonement,
which is the foundation of all practical piety and all
Christian hopes, must therefore be firmly established,

and defended against the fiery darts of Satan, with which it is attacked by innumerable adversaries.

Upon this subject, the opinions of divines may be classed under three heads: 1. That of the Socinians, who not only deny that an atonement was made, but affirm that it was not at all necessary, since God both could and would pardon sin, without any satisfaction made to his justice. 2. That of those who distinguish between an absolute and a hypothetical necessity; and in opposition to the Socinians maintain the latter, while they deny the former. By a hypothetical necessity they mean that which flows from the divine decree. God has decreed that an atonement is to be made, therefore it is necessary. To this they also add a necessity of fitness; as the commands of God have been transgressed, it is fit that satisfaction should be made, that the transgressor may not pass with impunity. Yet they deny that it was absolutely necessary, as God, they say, might have devised some other way of pardon than through the medium of an atonement. This is the ground taken by Augustine in his book on the Trinity. Some of the reformers who wrote before the time of Socinus, adopt the opinions of that father. 3. That of those who maintain its absolute necessity; affirming that God neither has willed, nor could have willed to forgive sins, without a satisfaction made to his justice. This, the common opinion of the orthodox, is our opinion.

Various errors are maintained on this point, by our opponents. The removal of the grounds upon which they rest will throw light upon the whole subject. They err in their views of the nature of sin, for which a satisfaction is required; of the satisfaction itself; of the character of God to whom it is to be rendered; and of Christ by whom it is rendered.

1. Of *sin*, which renders us guilty, and binds us over to punishment as hated of God. It may be viewed as a debt which we are bound to pay to divine justice, in which sense the law is called " a hand-writing," (Col. ii. 14:): as a principle of enmity, whereby we hate God and he becomes our enemy: as a crime against the government of the universe by which, before God, the supreme governor and judge, we become deserving of everlasting death and malediction. Whence, sinners are expressly called " debtors," (Matt. vi. 12); "enemies to God," both actively and passively, (Col. i. 21); "and guilty before God," (Rom. iii. 19.) We, therefore, infer that three things were necessary in order to our redemption; the payment of the debt contracted by sin, the appeasing of the divine wrath, and the expiation of guilt.

2. From the preceding remarks, the nature of the *satisfaction* which sin requires may be easily perceived. That which we are chiefly to attend to in sin being its criminality, satisfaction has relation to the penalty enacted against it by the Supreme Judge.

But here we must attend to a twofold payment, which is noticed by jurists. One which, by the very deed of payment, sets at liberty the debtor, and annuls the obligation, whether the payment is made by the debtor in his own person, or by a surety in his name. Another in which the bare fact of payment is not sufficient to liberate the debtor, because, the payment is not precisely that which is demanded in the obligation, but an equivalent. In this case, though the creditor has a right to refuse the acceptance of such payment, yet if he admits it and esteems it a payment, it is a satisfaction. The former of these takes place in a pecuniary, the latter in a penal debt. In a pecuniary transaction, the fact of the payment of the sum due frees the debtor, by whomsoever the payment is made. Respect here is had, not to the person paying, but to the payment only. Whence, the creditor, having been paid the full amount due, is not said to have treated with indulgence the debtor, or to have forgiven the debt. But in penal matters the case is different. The debt regards not things, but persons; not what is paid, so much as him who pays; i. e., that the transgressor may be punished. For as the law demands individual personal obedience, so it demands individual personal suffering. In order that the guilty person may be released through an atonement made by another in his stead, the governor or judge must pass a decree to that effect. That decree or act of the judge is, in relation to the law, called relaxation, and in relation to the debtor or guilty person, pardon; for his personal suffering is dispensed with, and in its place a vicarious suffering accepted. But because, in the subject under discussion, sin has not a relation to debt only, but also to punishment, satisfaction is not of that kind, which by the act itself frees the debtor. To effect this there must be an act of pardon passed by the Supreme Judge, because that is not precisely paid, i. e., a personal enduring of the penalty, which the law demands, but a vicarious suffering only. Hence we discover how perfectly accordant remission and satisfaction are with each other, notwithstanding the outcry made by the enemy respecting their supposed discrepancy. Christ made the *satisfaction* in his life and at his death, and God, by accepting this satisfaction, provides for *remission*. The satisfaction respects Christ, from whom God demands a punishment, not numerically, but in kind, the same with that which we owed. Pardon respects believers, who are freed from punishment in their own persons, while a vicarious suffering is accepted. Hence we see how admirably mercy is tempered with justice. Justice is exercised against sin, and mercy towards the sinner; an atonement is made to the divine justice by a surety, and God mercifully pardons us.

3. This reasoning is greatly fortified from a consideration of *the relations in which God stands to the sinner.*

He may be viewed in a threefold relation: as the creditor; as the Lord and party offended; and as the judge and ruler. But though both the former relations must be attended to in this matter, yet the third is to be chiefly considered. God here is not merely a creditor, who may at pleasure remit what is his due, nor merely the party offended who may do as he will with his own claims without injury to any one; but he is also a judge and rectoral governor, to whom alone pertains the infliction of punishment upon offenders, and the power of remitting the penal sanction of the law. This all jurists know belongs to the chief magistrate alone. The creditor may demand his debt, and the party offended reparation for the offence or indemnity for his loss; but the judge alone has the power to compel payment, or exact punishment. Here lies the capital error of our adversaries, who maintain that God is to be considered merely in the light of a creditor, who is at liberty to exact or remit the punishment at pleasure. It is however certain, that God sustains the character of judge and ruler of the world, who has the rights of sovereignty to maintain, and professes himself to be the guardian and avenger of his laws ; and hence he possesses not only the claims of a creditor, which he might assert or remit at pleasure, but also the right of government and of punishment, which is naturally indispensable. We must, however, in the punishment itself, distinguish accurately between the enforcing of the penalty, and the manner and circumstances under which it is enforced, as they are things widely different. Punishment may be viewed generally; and in this respect the right of Heaven to inflict it is indispensable, being founded in the divine justice. If there be such an attribute as justice belonging to God, then sin must have its due, which is punishment. But as to the manner and circumstances of the punishment, the case is altogether different. They are not essential to that attribute. They are to be arranged according to his will and pleasure. It may seem fit to the goodness of God that there should be, in relation to time, a delay of punishment; in relation to degree, a mitigation of it; and in relation to persons, a substitution. For although the person sinning deserves punishment and might suffer it with the strictest justice, yet such punishment is not necessarily indispensable. For reasons of great importance, it may be transferred to a surety. In this sense, it is said by divines that sin is of necessity punished impersonally, but every sinner is not therefore of necessity to be punished personally. Through the singular mercy of God some may be exempted from punishment, by the substitution of a surety in their stead.

But that we may conceive it possible for God to do this, he must not be considered as an inferior judge appointed by law. An officer of that character cannot remit anything of the rigour of the law by transferring the punishment from the actual offender to another person. God must be viewed in his true character, as a supreme judge who giveth account of none of his matters, who will satisfy his justice by the punishment of sin, and who, through his infinite wisdom and unspeakable mercy, determines to do this in such a way as shall relax somewhat of the extreme rigour of punishment, by admitting a substitute and letting the sinner go free. Hence we discover to whom the atonement is to be made ; whether to the devil, (as Socinus, with a sneer, asks,) or to God, as sovereign judge. For as the devil is no more than the servant of God, the keeper of the prison, who has no power over sinners, unless by the just judgment of God, the atonement is not to be made to this executor of the divine vengeance, but to the Supreme Ruler, who primarily and principally holds them in durance. We may add, that it is a gratuitous and false supposition, that in the suffering of punishment, there must be some person to whom the punishment shall be rendered, as in a pecuniary debt. It is sufficient that there is a judge, who may exact it in order to support the majesty of the State, and maintain the order of the empire.

4. The *person who makes the atonement* is here to be considered. As sin is to be viewed in the threefold light of debt, enmity, and crime ; and God in the

threefold light of creditor, party offended, and judge; so Christ must put on a threefold relation corresponding to all these. He must sustain the character of a Surety, for the payment of the debt. He must be a Mediator, a peace-maker, to take away the enmity of the parties and reconcile us to God. He must be a Priest and victim, to substitute himself in our room, and make atonement, by enduring the penal sanction of the law. Again: that such an atonement may be made, two things are requisite:—1. That the same *nature* which sins shall make restitution. 2. That the consideration given must possess infinite value, in order to the removal of the infinite demerit of sin. In Christ, two natures were necessary for the making of an atonement: a human nature, to suffer; and a divine nature, to give the requisite value to his sufferings.

Moreover, we must demonstrate how it is possible, in consistency with justice, to substitute an innocent person, as Christ was, in our room; because such a substitution, at first view, appears to be not only unusual, but also unjust. Though a substitution, which is common in a pecuniary debt, rarely occurs in penal transactions—nay, is sometimes prohibited, as was the case among the Romans, because no one is master of his own life, and because the commonwealth would suffer loss in such cases—yet it was not unknown among the heathen. We have an example of it in Damon and Pythias; two intimate friends, one of whom

1*

voluntarily entered himself bail for the other to Dionysius in a capital cause.   Curtius, Codrus, and Brutus devoted themselves for their country.   The right of punishing hostages, when princes fail in their promises, has been recognized by all nations.   Hence hostages are called ἀντίψυχοι, substitutes.   To this Paul alludes, when he says, (Rom. v. 7,) "For a good man some would even dare to die."   The Holy Scriptures often give it support, not only from the imputation of sin, by which one bears the punishment due to another, but from the public use of sacrifices, in which the victim was substituted in the place of the sinner and suffered death in his stead.   Hence the imposition of hands, and the confession of sins over the head of the victims.

But, that such a substitution may be made without the slightest appearance of injustice, various conditions are requisite in the substitute or surety, all which are found in Christ.   1. A common nature, that sin may be punished in the same nature which is guilty, (Heb. ii. 14.)   2. The consent of the will, that he should voluntarily take the burden upon himself, (Heb. x. 9,)—"*Lo, I come to do thy will.*"   3. Power over his own life, so that he may rightfully determine respecting it, (John, x. 18,)—"*No one taketh away my life, but I lay it down of myself, for I have power to lay it down, and take it up again.*"   4. The power of bearing the punishment due to us, and of freeing both himself and us from the power of death; because, if he himself could be holden of death, he could free no one from its dominion. That Christ possesses this power, no one doubts. 5. Holiness and immaculate purity, that, being polluted by no sin, he might not have to offer sacrifice for himself, but for us only, (Heb. vii. 26, 27.)

Under these conditions, it was not unjust for Christ to substitute himself in our room, while he is righteous and we unrighteous. By this act no injury is done to any one. Not to Christ, for he voluntarily took the punishment upon himself, and had the right to decide concerning his own life and death, and also power to raise himself from the dead. Not to God the judge, for he willed and commanded it; nor to his natural justice, for the Surety satisfied this by suffering the punishment which demanded it. Not to the empire of the universe, by depriving an innocent person of life, for Christ, freed from death, lives for evermore; or by the life of the surviving sinner injuring the kingdom of God, for he is converted and made holy by Christ. Not to the divine law, for its honour has been maintained by the perfect fulfilment of all its demands, through the righteousness of the Mediator; and, by our legal and mystical union, he becomes one with us, and we one with him. Hence he may justly take upon him our sin and sorrows, and impart to us his righteousness and blessings. So there is no abrogation of the law, no derogation from its claims ; as what we owed is transferred to the account of Christ, to be paid by him.

These preliminary remarks we have thought necessary, in order to the lucid discussion of the question concerning the necessity of the atonement. We now proceed to inquire whether it was necessary that Christ should satisfy for us, as well absolutely, in relation to the divine justice, as hypothetically, on the ground of a divine decree : whether it was absolutely necessary, in order to our salvation, that an atonement should be made, God not having the power to pardon our sins without a satisfaction, or whether it was rendered necessary only by the divine decree? The Socinians, indeed, admit no kind of necessity. Some of the old divines, and some members of the Reformed Church, contend for a hypothetical necessity only. They think it sufficient for the refutation of the heretic. But we, with the great body of the orthodox, contend for both. We do not urge a necessity simply natural, such as that of fire to burn, which is involuntary, and admits of no modification in its exercise. It is a moral and rational necessity for which we plead ; one which, as it flows from the holiness and justice of God, and cannot be exercised any other way than freely and voluntarily, admits of various modifications, provided there is no infringement of the natural rights of Deity. That there is such a necessity, is evinced by many arguments.

I. *The vindicatory justice of God.* That such an attribute is natural and essential to God, has been proved at large elsewhere. This avenging justice belongs to God as a judge, and he can no more dispense with it than he can cease to be a judge or deny himself; though, at the same time, he exercises it freely. It does not consist in the exercise of a gratuitous power, like mercy, by which, whether it be exercised or not, injustice is done to no one. It is that attribute by which God gives to every one his due, and from the exercise of which, when proper objects are presented, he can no more abstain, than he can do what is unjust. This justice is the constant will of punishing sinners, which in God cannot be inefficient, as his majesty is supreme and his power infinite. And hence the infliction of punishment upon the transgressor or his surety is inevitable. No objection to this can be drawn from the liberty of God, for that is exercised only in matters of positive enactment, not in such as are of natural right: nor from his mercy, because that, while it may free the sinner from punishment, does not demand that sin shall not be punished.

II. *The nature of sin,* which is a moral evil and essentially opposed to holiness, forms another argu-

ment.   The connection between it and physical evil is
natural and necessary.   As physical or penal evil
cannot exist without moral evil, either personal or
imputed, so there cannot be moral evil without pro-
ducing natural evil.   Moral and physical good, or
holiness and happiness, are united together by the wisdom, as well as by the goodness and justice of God;
so that a good man must be happy, for goodness is a
part of the divine image.   The wicked must be miserable, because God is just; and this the rather, because
when God gives blessings to the righteous, he does it
of his own bounty, without any merit on their part;
but when he punishes the sinner, he renders to him
precisely what he has merited by his sins.

III. *The sanction of the Law*, which threatens death
to the sinner, (Deut. xxvii. 29. Gen. ii. 17. Ez. xviii.
20. Rom. i. 18, 32, and vi. 23.) Since God is true
and cannot lie, these threatenings must necessarily be
executed either upon the sinner, or upon some one in
his stead.   In vain do our opponents reply, that the
threatening is hypothetical, not absolute, and may be
relaxed by repentance.   This is a gratuitous supposition.   That such a condition is either expressed or
understood, neither has been nor can be proved.
Nay, as the penal sanction of the law is a part of the
law itself, which is natural and indispensable, this
sanction must also be immutable.   With the judicial
threatenings of the law, we must not confound par-

ticular and economical comminations, or such as are
paternal and evangelical, which are denounced against
men to recal them to repentance. Such threatenings
may be recalled in case of penitence. Of this kind
were those denounced against Hezekiah, (Isaiah
xxxviii.) and against Nineveh, (Jon. iii.)

IV. *The Preaching of the Gospel*, which announces
the violent and painful death of the Mediator and
Surety on the cross, is another argument which powerfully confirms the necessity of that event. For we
cannot believe that God would multiply sufferings
unnecessarily. His goodness and wisdom do not per-
mit us to harbour an idea that the Father could expose his most innocent and beloved Son to an excruciating and ignominious death, without a necessity
which admits of no relaxation. The only necessity
which can be possibly imagined here, is that of making
an atonement to the divine justice for our sins.
Every one must perceive that it was absolutely necessary. I know that our opponents affect to produce
various other reasons for the accursed death of the
cross, such as to confirm Christ's doctrine, and to set
an example of all kinds of virtue, especially of charity
and constancy! But since Christ had confirmed his
doctrines by numerous stupendous miracles, and
through his life had given the most illustrious examples of every human virtue, who could believe that
God, for that one cause alone, would expose his only-

begotten Son to such dire torments? Therefore, without all doubt, there was another cause for that dispensation, to wit: a regard for the honour of his justice. To this the Holy Spirit bears witness by the Apostle Paul, (Rom. iii. 5,) who affirms that " God hath set forth Christ *to be a propitiation for our sins—εις ἔνδειξιν της δικαιοσυνη ἀντου—to declare his righteousness*," which was inexorable, and did not suffer our sins to be pardoned on any other terms, than by the intervention of the death of Christ.

Again: if God was able and willing by his word alone without any atonement to pardon our sins, why does the Apostle Paul so often and emphatically refer our justification and salvation to the blood of Christ? " *We are justified by the redemption which is in his blood,*" (Rom. iii. 24.) " *We have redemption through his blood; the remission of sins,*" (Eph. i. 7.) " *He hath reconciled all things to himself by the blood of Christ,*" (Col. i. 20.) Now there was no need that his blood should be shed if remission depended solely upon the divine will. On this supposition, the apostle would rashly and falsely affirm, what he often affirms, that the blood of bulls and of goats, that is, the sacrifices under the law, could not take away sins; and that the oblation of Christ alone could. If there was no need of any purgation, but penitence alone was sufficient to *take away sin*, that is, the guilt of sin, without any sacrifice, the apostle's assertion is groundless. What could be taken away without any sacrifice at all, could surely be removed by legal sacrifices. If the divine will alone is necessary, why is it that Paul never refers to it, but always ascends to the nature of things, as when he asserts that it was impossible for the blood of bulls to take away sins? Surely it must be because sin is so hateful to God, that its stain can be washed away by nothing less than the blood of the Son of God.

V. If there was no necessity that Christ should die, *the greatness of God's love* in not sparing his own Son, but delivering him up for us all, which the apostle commends, will be not a little diminished. If there was no obstacle on the part of justice, in the way of our salvation, it would indeed have been great grace in God to have forgiven our sins. But it would have fallen far short of that stupendous love which, though justice inexorable stood in the way, removed, by means found in the treasures of infinite wisdom, all impediments to our redemption, displaying a most amiable harmony between justice and mercy. Nor can Christ be said to have appeased the wrath of God, if he, without demanding any satisfaction, could by a mere volition have laid aside his own wrath.

VI. Finally, our opinion relative to the necessity of an atonement does not, in the least, derogate from any *of the Divine Perfections.* Not from God's absolute Power, because he can neither deny himself nor any of his attributes, nor can he act in such a way as to give the appearance of delighting in sin, by holding communion with the sinner.   Not from the Freedom of his Will, because he can will nothing contrary to his justice and holiness, which would be injured should sin go unpunished.   Not from his boundless Mercy, for this is exercised towards the sinner, though punishment is inflicted on the Surety.   On the contrary, it makes a glorious display of the most illustrious of the divine perfections: of his Holiness, on account of which he can have no communion with the sinner, until, by an atonement, his guilt is removed and his pollution purged; of his Justice, which inexorably demands punishment of sin; of his Wisdom, in reconciling the respective claims of justice and mercy; and of his Love, in not sparing his own Son in order that he might spare us.

CHAPTER II.

𝕿𝖍𝖊 𝕿𝖗𝖚𝖙𝖍 𝖔𝖋 𝖙𝖍𝖊 𝕬𝖙𝖔𝖓𝖊𝖒𝖊𝖓𝖙.

STATEMENT OF THE QUESTION.—ARGUMENTS FOR THE TRUTH OF THE ATONEMENT:—I. CHRIST IS SAID TO HAVE REDEEMED HIS PEOPLE AT THE PRICE OF HIS BLOOD.—II. HE DIED IN THEIR PLACE.—III. HE BORE THEIR SINS.—IV. HE OFFERED A SACRIFICE ON THE CROSS.— V. HE MADE RECONCILIATION WITH GOD.—VI. THE NATURE OF HIS DEATH.—VII. THE PERFECTIONS OF GOD.—OBJECTIONS ANSWERED:—THAT THE WORD SATISFACTION IS NOT USED IN SCRIPTURE;—THAT CHRIST'S SUFFERINGS ARE EXEMPLARY;—THAT SATISFACTION AND REMISSION ARE INCONSISTENT WITH EACH OTHER;— THAT ON OUR SUPPOSITION CHRIST MUST HAVE MADE SATISFACTION TO HIMSELF;—THAT HE DID NOT SUFFER ETERNAL DEATH;—THAT HE DID NOT SUFFER DESPAIR;—THAT THE DEATH OF ONE COULD NOT JUSTLY ANSWER FOR THE DEATH OF MANY;—THAT ATONEMENT IS OPPOSED TO EZEKIEL XVIII. 20; AND THAT IT LEADS TO SIN AND CARNAL EASE.

HAVING in the last chapter asserted the necessity of the atonement, we shall now endeavour to prove its truth, which the Socinians not only call in question, but expressly deny. Though, in order to conceal their real views, they appear willing to retain the word satisfaction, and indeed often use it, yet it is in a sense widely different from that of the orthodox divines; as will appear from the statement of the question.

The subject in controversy is not, whether Christ,

by a general satisfaction, has fulfilled all the conditions which the divine will imposed upon him, in order to procure our salvation; for our adversaries admit such a satisfaction, as Crellius professes in his book against Grotius.   But we inquire whether the satisfaction made by Christ was strictly penal, and not only fulfilled the will of God, but also satisfied his justice; Christ having taken upon himself our sins.   Our opponents deny; we affirm.

The controversy does not respect a metaphorical satisfaction, which is effected by a nominal remission of sin; a satisfaction, which by supplication obtains, through the mere indulgence of God, some favour. This is admitted, and often spoken of by our adversaries to deceive the simple.   But they pertinaciously deny that Christ has made a true and proper satisfaction, by paying a full price, and by obtaining, through his merits, the acquittal of the sinner on the ground of justice.   We maintain that this is the true scriptural atonement.

It is not whether the death of Christ is advantageous to us, and in various respects promotes our interests; for this also they willingly admit.   It is whether, by substituting himself in our place, he suffered the punishment due to us.   We maintain that he did.

It is not whether Christ is our Saviour, on account of his doctrine announcing to us the way of salvation; on account of the example of his life, in which by his virtues and miracles he confirmed the truth; or on account of his efficacious power, by which he will assuredly bestow on us this salvation; for all this Socinus* grants to Christ. The great subject of debate is, whether Christ, by his satisfaction and merits, is our Saviour in the strictest sense of the word. Our opponents have openly made the utmost exertions to overturn this doctrine, which has been constantly held by the orthodox, and is proved by various solid and irresistible arguments.

I. The first argument is drawn from those texts in which Christ is said *to have redeemed us at the price of his blood;* for the payment of a price properly so called and perfectly sufficient, shows that a satisfaction in its true and proper sense has been made, since price always has reference to distributive justice. These texts are various. " *Ye were redeeemed by a price.*"† " *Ye were redeemed from your vain conversation, not by corruptible things such as silver and gold, but by the precious blood of Christ, as of a lamb without spot.*"‡ " *Christ gave himself for us, that he might redeem (purchase) us from all iniquity.*"§ " *In whom we have redemption through his blood.*"‖ " *The Son of man came that he might lay down his life a ransom for many*—λυτρον αντι πολλῶν— i. e., a price of payment, in the room of many. The name

---

* Chap. 9, Book I. de Servatore, Chap. 5, 6.   † 1 Cor. vi. 20.
‡ 1 Pet. i. 19.   § Tit. ii. 14.   ‖ Eph. i. 7.

Jesus was given to him, "because he saves his people from their sins."*

Though the word *Redemption* is sometimes used in Scripture to denote a mere deliverance, which is procured without the payment of any price, as Moses is called λυτρωτης, a deliverer;† and as God is said to have "redeemed Israel out of the house of bondage;" yet it does not follow that in this argument it is to be taken in that sense.   Many things prove that in the business of man's salvation, the word is to be understood as signifying redemption by the payment of a price.   1. This is the primary import of the words λυτρον, απολυτρον, and we may in no case give them any other, unless for a very solid reason.   This is not denied by Socinus himself.‡   "To redeem any one, properly signifies nothing else but to free a captive, by paying a price to him who detains him."   2. The condition of man requires this; since he is a prisoner not only of Satan and death, but also of sin, both as to its guilt and its pollution, and therefore of the divine law and justice. He is condemned of God and a child of wrath, and cannot be released but by a satisfactory payment.   3. Such is the redemption procured by the price mentioned, (1 Cor. vi. 20.)   Why should the apostle use λυτρον and τιμη, price of redemption and punishment, if no price was

* Matt. i. 21.   † Acts, vii. 35.   Deut. vii. 8.
‡ Book xii. chap. i.

paid? The reply usually made to this is, that the term is used in a figurative sense, and denotes that we are freed from the power of sin. This is an assumption, which, as we do not grant it, our opponent is bound to prove. Nay, the contrary is evident. The price is compared to very precious earthly things, such as gold, silver, and jewels, which have always a relation to price, strictly so called, (1 Pet. i. 18.) 4 We have not only the word λυτρον, a price of redemption, but also the word αντιλυτρον, applied to the suffering and death of Christ. Nothing can be more express than this word αντιλυτρον. It denotes not merely a price, but such a price as is perfectly equal to the debt which it pays; this is the force of the preposition αντι, which here expresses substitution. Aristotle uses the same word αντιλυτρον, in the 9th book of his Ethics, and 2d chapter, to denote the redemption of a life, by substituting another in its room.

Hence it appears that this redemption is not a mere manumission, such as that in which a master, without any price, sets free his slaves; nor is it simply an act of power, by which captives are rescued from the hand of an enemy; nor a bare exchange, such as that of prisoners of war. It is a real satisfaction, such as a surety makes by paying in full for the debtor. Our deliverance, indeed, is procured without any price paid on our part, and purely through the free grace and

mercy of God.* The divine power, too, is displayed
gloriously in emancipating us from the tyrannical dominion of Satan, over whom Christ obtains a victory
and triumph.† There is also an exchange in respect
of Christ, who was substituted in our place, and suffered the punishment due to us. Yet in relation to
the justice of God there is a real and perfect satisfaction made.

II. The truth of the atonement is also proved from
those passages of Scripture, in which Christ is *said to
have died,* not only for our advantage, but also *in our
stead, as a substitute.* " *For when we were yet without
strength, in due time Christ died for the ungodly—in that
while we were yet sinners, Christ died for us.*"‡ " *For
Christ also hath suffered for our sins, the just for the unjust.*"§ Our reasons for understanding these phrases in
this sense and none other, are: 1. This is the common
import of the preposition υπερ, (for,) which is used in
these texts, and which, when applied to persons, denotes
among the Greeks substitution: as in Romans, v. 7:
" Scarcely for a just man will one die," i. e., in his
place; and in Romans, xi. 3, " αναθεμα υπερ αδελφων,"
" for or in the room of his brethren." 2. It is elsewhere expressed by αντι, in the room of, as in Matt.

---

* Rom. iii. 24. Eph. ii. 8,   † Col. ii. 15.
‡ Rom. v. 6, 7.   § 1 Pet. iii. 18.

xx. 28, and by *αντιλυτρον*, a price of redemption, as in
1 Tim. ii. 6. " *Who gave himself a ransom* (*αντιλυτρον*)
for all." Both of these import substitution; life for
life, as in the phrase " *eye for* (*αντι*) *eye*."* 3. Christ
is said to have died for us in a manner peculiar to
himself—a manner in which neither Paul nor Peter
could be said to die or be crucified for us.† Yet either
of these might be said to die for our edification and
confirmation in the faith. Hence the sufferings and
death of Christ were vicarious ; and in their design
entirely different from that of the apostles or martyrs. Though the apostles may be said to have
suffered for the Church, yet it does not follow from
this, that the object of their death was the same with
that of Christ's. They suffered as martyrs, to edify,
confirm, and comfort the Church, by bearing testimony
to the truth of the Christian system ; as it is expressed by the apostle : "*Whether we be afflicted, it is
for your consolation;*"‡ but Christ alone laid down his
life to redeem the Church. And if we are commanded to lay down our lives for our brethren,§ as
Christ laid down his life for us, this means that we
are not to refuse to undergo the danger of death, nay,
to suffer with firmness even death itself, whenever the
glory of God, the good of our neighbour, or the edifi-

* Matt. v. 38. † 1 Cor. i. 13.
‡ 2 Cor. i. 6. § 1 John, iii. 13.

2

cation of the Church requires it, as was the case with
the martyrs. Hence, indeed, we may infer that we
should in this way imitate the example of Christ; but
it does not hence follow, that our death for our brethren is for the same purposes as Christ's death for us.
We are unable to pay a ransom for our brother, that
we may free him from death, as the Psalmist expresses
it in Psalm xlix. 8 : nor by our death can we procure
his reconciliation with God and purge him from sin—
all which Christ does for his people by his death. Thus
our death may in some respects be compared to that
of Christ, but not in all. In relation to an example
of love, a comparison may be instituted, but not in
relation to the merit of satisfaction. The particle
καθως, *as*, denotes similitude, not equality, as may be
learned from its use in Matt. v. 48: "*Be ye perfect,
even as (καθως) your Father in heaven is perfect.*"

III. Another proof is derived from those Scriptures in which Christ is said *to have borne our sins*, and
on account of them to have been afflicted, to have
been wounded, to have died. "*He bore our sins in his
own body on the tree.*"* This passage is taken by the
apostle from the 53d chapter of Isaiah, in which the
Chaldee Paraphrase and the ancient Jews consider

* 1 Pet. ii. 24.

the prophet as treating of Messiah. *"He hath borne our griefs and carried our sorrows—he was wounded for our transgressions, he was bruised for our iniquities—the chastisement of our peace was upon him—the Lord hath laid on him the iniquity* (i. e., the punishment) *of us all—he shall make his soul an offering for sin."*

In proving the atonement from these texts, we reason as follows:—1. *From bearing our sins:* though to bear and to carry are sometimes figuratively put for taking away and pardoning,* yet there is no good reason why we thus should understand them in these passages. Nay, there are most weighty reasons which forbid us to depart from the primary and most common signification, according to which, as Socinus himself acknowledges,† to bear sin, is the same thing as to bear the punishment of sin. The word נשא, which sometimes relates to a simple taking away of sin, is indeed used; but the word סבל, which signifies the bearing of a burden laid upon one, is also used, and clearly intimates the suffering of punishment. 2. The *manner of bearing the sins* confirms us in this view. The sins are borne by the bearer's being bruised and wounded. Sin is also said *to be laid upon him.* None of these could be said, unless Christ took upon himself and suffered the punishment of sin. 3. Christ made his soul an offering, and laid

---

* Exod. xxxiv. 7, and Numb. xiv. 18. † Prælec. cap. 21.

down his life an offering for sin, *bore sin in the manner of a victim;* nay, he made himself in reality a victim by suffering death and shedding his blood in the room of sinners. 4. All things which indicate a real satisfaction occur in this portion of Scripture: our sins as the moving, the meritorious cause, " *he was bruised for our iniquities,*" v. 4, 5, 6 : the suffering of punishment due to sin ; " *he hath borne our griefs, and carried our sorrows,*" v. 4: the imputation of our sins to Christ by God as a judge ; " *the Lord laid on him the iniquity of us all,*" v. 6: the voluntary undertaking of Christ as our surety; " *he was oppressed and afflicted, yet he opened not his mouth,*" in complaining of his sufferings, or in refusing to bear them, v. 8: an expiation for sin and a full payment of the debt ; " *yet it pleased the Lord to bruise him; he hath put him to grief: when thou shalt make his soul on offering for sin,*" v. 8, 10. Now, with what propriety could all these things be affirmed, if Christ laid down his life merely to exhibit an example of patience and love, and not to make satisfaction for sin ?

In Matt. viii. 17, we are, indeed, informed that this prophecy of Isaiah was fulfilled, when Christ healed bodily diseases, which, properly speaking, he did not bear, but take away; yet we cannot infer from this, that the same thing may be affirmed of sins which are the diseases of the mind ; for the diseases of the body are to be viewed in a different light from those

of the mind. In healing the former, it was not necessary that Christ should himself become sick; it was
only necessary that he should exercise his power.
Not so the latter. He must first take them upon
himself before he could take them away from us.
Hence he is held forth by the prophet as wounded
and bruised, which were not necessary to the healing
of bodily maladies, but to bearing those of the mind
alone; from which it is easy to infer what the mind
of the Holy Spirit is in this prophecy, and how it is
said to have been fulfilled when Christ healed corpo-
ral diseases. Without doubt, it relates primarily to
spiritual disease and debility, i. e., to sin, the punishment of which was laid upon him, that he might
suffer its desert in our room. But bodily infirmities
and pains are a part of the punishment of sin, and on
this account, in a secondary and subordinate sense, it
refers to them; because Christ had a right to heal
them. Thus, what the prophet declares in general
concerning all diseases, Peter applies in particular to
the diseases of the mind, and Matthew to the diseases
of the body, not excluding, but rather including, those
of the mind. He demonstrates that by removing the
cause the effect was taken away. Spiritual and
physical maladies are intimately connected with each
other; the former draw after them the latter, while
the latter presuppose the former. Christ is said to
have borne both, but in different ways, according to

their different natures. Bodily griefs he bore only
by efficaciously taking them away, not by undergoing
them in his own person ; but he bore spiritual griefs
in two methods : by suffering them himself, and by
taking them away. Nor, if Matthew asserts that
Christ healed the sick, and thus fulfilled this prophecy, may we thence rightly infer that the Spirit refers
to them alone ; because it is well known, that in the
Scriptures, a prophecy is said to be accomplished, not
only when it is completely and ultimately fulfilled,
but also when a partial accomplishment of it is
begun.

Here also are to be considered those Scriptures
which assert that Christ was made sin and a curse for
us.* How can he be said " *to have been made sin*," i. e.,
an offering for sin, by God as a judge ; and a " *curse*,"
i. e., a subject of the malediction which the law pronounces against sinners ; not, indeed, for himself, seeing
he was most holy and supremely beloved by his Father,
but *for us;* unless it was as being substituted in our
place, and taking upon himself that curse which the law
justly pronounces against our sins, in order that he
might bear it, and by bearing it take it away?   Thus
he was made a blessing, by procuring for us the remission of our sins and a right to eternal life.   What
reference is there here to an example of patience, or

* Gal. iii. 13, and 2 Cor. v. 21.   Lev. viii. 9.

to a confirmation of doctrine? Is it not most evident
that there was a real substitution of Christ in our
room; and that in consequence of this substitution, a
real satisfaction, expiation or atonement has been
made, and that this is the doctrine taught by these
Scriptural phrases? The force of this argument cannot be evaded by objecting that Christ is said to have
been a curse, not on account of having really borne
the curse of the law, which could not have been laid
on him, a perfectly blessed and holy person; but because he suffered crucifixion, which, under the law,
was denominated a curse. The very words of the
apostle, and the redemption from the curse of the law,
which Christ by his death procured for us, evince the
futility of the objection. How can he be a curse, and
that for the express purpose of delivering us from the
curse, unless he took it upon himself? It is no solid
objection to this reasoning, that he is the only-begotten Son, and the ever-blessed God; for he did not endure the curse, in and for himself as the Son of God,
but as our surety and on our behalf. Hence as to his
person, he is styled " blessed forever," and in his offi-
cial character as our representative, he is said to have
suffered the punishment due to our sins.

Hence we are enabled to understand the force of
the expression, *" he was delivered for our offences."**

* Rom. iv. 25.

Socinus contends, that all which is here intended, is, that an *occasion* for the death of Christ was given by our offences, or that Christ died only with the view that he might, by his example, incline us to leave off the commission of sin, and render us certain of its pardon. All which is incompatible with the Scriptures quoted above, which teach us that the meritorious and moving cause, for Christ's being delivered over to death, was our sins, that he might suffer the punishment due to them and take away their guilt. He is said "*to have been delivered for our offences,*" as sacrifices were offered for sin, doubtless, on account of its guilt and to take it away. Hence the guilt of our sins was the meritorious cause of the death of Christ, and its final cause or chief end, to expiate and remove this guilt.

IV. The truth of the atonement is further proved, from *the sacrifice of Christ* on the cross, of which the Scriptures so often speak.* Why should Christ be so often and so expressly called a priest, truly and properly a priest, far more excellent than all the Levitical priests, one who by his oblation appeased the wrath of God, and obtained eternal salvation for us; unless because a full expiation for sin has been made

---

* Isai. liii. 10, John i. 29, Eph. vi. 2, and the Epistle to the Hebrews, *passim.*

by his satisfaction, and a more luminous display
of the truths shadowed forth by the ancient figures?
As by the sacrifices under the law, doctrines were not
confirmed, examples of love and obedience were not
given, no covenant was entered into, nor could they
by their own efficacy appease the wrath of God; these
sacrifices must have been instituted with a primary
view to represent a real satisfaction, an atoning sacrifice for sin. This is more particularly confirmed:
1. From the nature of the priesthood which Christ sustains. He is constituted a priest in things pertaining
to God, to appease him by an atoning sacrifice. 2. From
the nature of the victim which is substituted in the
room of sinners, to bear the punishment of death due
to them, as evinced by the rite of imposing hands upon
the head of the offering, and over it making a confession of sin. 3. From the threefold effect of the sacrifice: in respect to God, by the propitiation of his wrath;
in respect to sin, by the expiation and removal of its
guilt; in respect to man, by the pardon which followed
from the propitiation of God and the expiation of sin.
For a person cannot be freed and obtain pardon, without the substitution of a victim in his room; nor can
God be appeased without the shedding of blood; nor
can sin be expiated without the suffering of punishment.

The objections which Volkelius and others oppose
to this reasoning, do not, in the least, weaken its force.

2*

They object: (1.) "That the propitiatory sacrifices did not all prefigure the sacrifice of Christ; but the annual sacrifice only, which was offered upon the great day of expiation, and which contained no satisfaction; as a satisfaction could flow neither from the victims offered up nor from the person of the chief priest." The Apostle Paul, on whose judgment more dependence is to be placed than on that of our opponents, opposes not one propitiatory sacrifice only, but all the sacrifices to that of Christ, and hence he infers their abrogation.* Neither the perpetual sacrifice offered up daily, nor the other propitiatory offerings of lambs which were of a private nature, could refer to anything else than the oblation of the immaculate Lamb of God for us. It is no objection to this view, that they were offered for individuals, and not for all in common; for, as the sacrifices which were offered for the whole congregation of Israel, signified that Christ was to make a propitiation for the sins of all his people, so those which were offered for each individual, were designed to show that every one of Christ's people laden with sin, should seek and obtain reconciliation through the offering of Christ. Further, although those sacrifices did not, in the sight of God, contain a satisfaction properly so called; because the soul of man is of too exalted a value to be purchased with the blood of bulls

* Heb. vii. 27, and x. 4, 5, 11.

or of goats: yet a typical, ceremonial satisfaction, pertaining to the purity of the flesh, was made by them,* a satisfaction, which by the appointment of God was to be attributed, neither to the victims, nor to the officiating priest separately, but jointly to both.

Another objection is that: (2.) "An expiation is nothing else than an entire deliverance from the dominion of sin, which deliverance cannot be in the way of merit attributed to the death of Christ, but only in the way of example and declaratively." In this objection, the cause is confounded with the effect. The office of the judge, who releases the prisoner, is confounded with the office of the surety, who pays the ransom. The judge sets the prisoner at liberty, while the prisoner, or some one in his place, pays the price of his redemption. Hence it follows that the purging of guilt and the removal of the accusation are effected by the suffering of punishment either in the person of the accused, or in that of another. If all the end answered by the death of Christ was to declare that an expiation was to be made, it effected nothing more than the victims under the law, which might, nay did attest the same thing; yet the Apostle Paul expressly declares that they could not make expiation for sin. If there were any propriety in this objection, the expiation might be attributed no less to Christ's resur-

* Heb. ix. 13.

rection than to his death, which the Scripture nowhere does. Besides, declaration respects men, expiation God; that belongs rather to his prophetical office, this to his priestly. Though the work of expiation may sometimes be attributed to God the Father,* who never makes satisfaction, yet we cannot justly infer that this expiation is of the same nature with that of Christ; because, according to the different nature of the subjects to whom the expiation is attributed, it is to be differently understood. For God the Father to expiate, is to admit of an expiation made by a priest, which is done by pardon and acceptance. But for a priest and victim to expiate, is to effect reconciliation meritoriously by the shedding of blood and vicarious suffering.

It is further objected that: (3.) "Sacrifices were offered up only for smaller offences, such as were committed through ignorance or error; while for more aggravated, wilful transgressions, there were no sacrifices instituted; but that Christ died for all sins without distinction." This objection is grounded on an assumption which we do not admit. It is indeed expressly contrary to Scripture. On the great day of annual atonement, the goat is said to bear all the iniquities of the children of Israel. Sacrifices are elsewhere said to be offered up not for those sins only which are committed through error, but for those

* Deut. xxi. 8.

which are committed willingly, and which are expressed by פשע, אשם הטא, פעל, and similar words.*
And though the priest is said to have offered for
the errors (αγνοηματων) of the people,† yet it does
not follow that wilful sins are excluded; for the word
αγνοημα, which signifies properly an error of the mind,
is used to denote every kind of sin, because every sin
proceeds from an error of the mind.   Hence wickod
men are called foolo, ανοητοι.   The Septuagint renders
פשע and אשם by the Greek word αγνοια, and these
Hebrew words signify wickedness and rebellion.
For some aggravated crimes, such as murder, idolatry,
adultery, etc., we do not read of any sacrifices having
been particularly instituted; because God determined
to punish them by the sword of the civil magistrate
with capital punishment; and those who sinned thus
had no need of this remedy, as their death was a satisfaction to the public.

V. Again, we argue for the doctrine of the atonement, *from our reconciliation with God*, which Christ by
his death has procured for us. Since that reconciliation supposes the making up of the breach which sin
had produced between God and his creatures, this
could not be effected without the removal of a twofold barrier, by a satisfaction.   On the part of God,

* Lev. xvi. 21, 22.   † Heb. ix. 6, 7.

his justice must be satisfied, and on the part of man, the guilt of sin must be removed by suffering the punishment due to it.   The Apostle Paul, everywhere, teaches us that Christ procured for us such a reconciliation.*

The substance of the objections which our opponents offer against this argument is, that " this reconciliation is effected by our conversion to God, and not at all by appeasing the divine wrath, because God is not said to be reconciled to us, but we to God; nay, he is said to procure for us this reconciliation, which is not the part of an enemy, but of a friend."   This capital error of our opponents is refuted by many powerful arguments.   1. The Scriptures speak of a double enmity and reconciliation, not only on the part of man, who by sin is become a hater of God,† an enemy in his mind by wicked works;‡ but also on the part of God, by his wrath which is revealed from heaven against all iniquity.§   Hence men are by nature children of wrath.‖   God is said to be of purer eyes than to behold iniquity.¶   He hates all workers of iniquity.**   Now as there is an alienation on both sides, so there must be on each side a reconciliation: on the part of God, by a turning away of his wrath; on the

---

* Rom. v. 10.   2 Cor. v. 18, 19.   Col. i. 20, 21, &c.

† Rom. i. 21.   ‡ Col. i. 21.   § Rom. i. 18.

‖ Eph. ii. 5.   ¶ Hab. i. 13.   ** Psalm v. 5.

part of man, by a conversion to God: all which the Apostle clearly teaches, (2 Cor., v. 18, 19.) In consequence of God's reconciling us to himself through Christ, Paul shows that the apostles, in the name of Christ, exhorted sinners to be reconciled to God. 2. If reconciliation were nothing but conversion, then it should rather be said to proceed from Christ's holy life, than from his bloody death. On this ground, no reason can be offered why the Apostle should propose sanctification as the end of our reconciliation,* for nothing can be the medium and end of itself. This would be to say that the end of reconciliation was reconciliation. 3. It is such a reconciliation as is effected by not imputing to us our sins, on account of their having been imputed to Christ, who was made sin for us;† a reconciliation effected by the substitution of Christ in our place, that he might die for us; as we collect from the comparison instituted between him and the man who would dare to die for a good man;‡ which implies a proper satisfaction, not a simple conversion. 4. This reconciliation is effected "*by making peace through the blobd of his cross,*"§ and by an atoning sacrifice, ιλασμος.‖ All these denote not mere conversion; but primarily, the appeasing of the divine wrath, which is effected by the death of a victim.

---

* Col. i. 22. † 2 Cor. v. 18, 21. ‡ Rom. v. 7.
§ Col. i. 20. ‖ 1 John, ii. 2.

Though the Scriptures commonly speak of our being reconciled to God, rather than of God's being reconciled to us, because those who offend have need to be reconciled to him who is offended; yet this, so far from excluding the reconciliation of God to us, includes it; because there can be no offence, unless justice is injured; and this injury must be repaired before God can reconcile men to himself, and admit them to hold communion with him. God's procuring this reconciliation for us, is no evidence that he has not been angry with us, or that he was at peace and in a state of friendship with us. It only proves that God, moved towards us with a love of benevolence, decreed to procure for us a reconciliation; not that he was forthwith to be deemed appeased and reconciled, but only that he might become so, while yet, in the mean time, he could not but be offended at our sins.

In vain is it pleaded by our opponents, that " Christ is said to be our propitiation and expiatory sacrifice; not that he may reconcile an angry God to us, but that he may testify that God is already appeased and by no means angry with us." The blood of Christ was not shed to prove the remission of sin, but to obtain it, as was the case in the propitiatory sacrifices under the Old Testament dispensation; otherwise, there was no need that Christ should die and shed his blood, when the truth of the remission could be as well attested by his life and doctrine. Nor because the covering of the ark is improperly and declaratively called ιλαστηριον, or an expiation, because by it God declared his benevolence towards his people, are we thence to infer that it was of the same nature with the expiation made by Christ. The making of expiation is attributed to Christ not so much passively as actively, and in the strictest sense of the word. What was only typically and symboli cally shadowed forth In the mercy-seat and by the sprinkling of the blood of victims, Christ truly and properly effected by the shedding of his own blood. Again: though the application and fruit of this atonement is imparted to us through the medium of his continual intercession in heaven, yet we may not hence infer that he has made it in heaven only. The passage in Heb. ii. 17 does not relate to this; for it is not there said that he makes reconciliation for the sins of the people in heaven, but only that he must be made like unto his brethren in all things, that he may be a faithful high priest, in things pertaining to God, and in this character make reconciliation, which he had done by his death and suffering, as is intimated in the following verse.

VI. The doctrine of the atonement is also confirmed by *the nature and circumstances of Christ's passion*, as well as by *the kind of death* which he suffered; in all which we have everything requisite to a full and perfect satisfaction. (Let us consider the essence and kind of the punishment. The death which he endured was not a common death; but violent and most bitter, inflicted as a punishment, and accursed of God himself; one in which he suffered the greatest ignominy and experienced the severest pains in his most holy body. His soul was seized with the most appalling terror and sorrow, with such fear and anguish that an angel was sent to minister comfort to him. Sweat flowed from the pores of his body like great drops of blood, and " he offered up prayers and supplications, with strong crying and tears to him who was able to save him."* With a voice of deepest sadness, he complained that he was forsaken by God the Father, though not by a dissolution of the union, nor by withdrawing a participation of holiness, nor by withholding his supporting power, yet by withholding from him the beatific vision, by suspending the sense and fruition of full felicity. How shall we find an adequate cause for all these sufferings in a perfectly holy person, unless by admitting that avenging justice demanded from Christ a full atonement for our sins? Or shall we say that Christ was of more feeble mind and possessed less heroic firmness, than innumerable martyrs, who have suffered the same most painful death of the cross,

* Heb. v. 7.

nay, if possible, torments more intolerable, and yet with unshaken fortitude, with the greatest alacrity, and without any indications of grief or terror? Such blasphemy shocks the ears of the Christian. Though the time of Christ's sufferings was but finite in duration, yet, in consequence of the dignity of the sufferer, it was equal in value to infinite duration of torment. The law, indeed, demands that the person who sins shall suffer; but the Gospel, through the fatherly kindness of God, declares it meet that there shall be a substitution; that it suffices to punish sin, and let the sinner go free.)

VII. A final argument is drawn from the *Perfections of God*. By the atonement we have an astonishing display of the divine *Mercy*, which is so great that God spared not his own Son, that he might spare us. It asserts the claims of *Justice*, which, that it might remain unimpeachable, demanded even the blood of the Son of God. It gloriously exhibits the divine *Wisdom*, which found out an admirable plan of reconciling mercy with justice, and untied a knot which otherwise could never have been loosed; a plan by which the conscience of man, alarmed with a penetrating sense of sin, judgment, and the divine malediction, is rendered peaceful and serene. Take away the atonement, and what becomes of the *Truth* of God, which so uniformly denounces death and a curse against sinners? What becomes of justice, which not only acquits the guilty and convicted sinner without inflicting upon him the deserved punishment, but also bestows on him rewards most honourable? Besides, by denying the atonement, the following absurdities are unavoidable:—1. That our redemption may be attributed no less to the death of the apostles and martyrs than to the death of Christ; since, by their death and sufferings, they have given strong testimony in favour of the doctrines of the Gospel, and have set before us in their lives illustrious examples of patience and obedience. 2. That Christ saved us rather by his life and miracles than by his death, since the promulgation of his doctrines and the example of his life were much more plain exhibitions of truth than his death affords. 3. The priestly office is altogether taken away from this world, and confounded with his prophetical and kingly offices. 4. The saints under the Old Testament were not saved by Christ; because they had not the benefit of his example, nor did they hear him preaching doctrines.

We now proceed to remove the difficulties which have been raised.

Though the word satisfaction is not expressly used in the Scriptures, yet, what is quite sufficient, there are other words used which are altogether equivalent to it, and which either have no meaning or else mean that real satisfaction for which we contend. Such are the words *απολυτρωσις*, the redemption of a captive, by making a payment; *αντιλυτρον*, a price of redemption; *ιλασμος*, a propitiation; *τιμη*, a price of punishment; *καταρα*, a curse; *θυσια*, a sacrifice; *προσφορα*, an offering; and many others of the same import, which we have mentioned above.

As Christ sustains a twofold relation to believers—one in the character of their Surety, bound to satisfy justice in their behalf; the other in the character of their Head and Lord, operating in them by the animating and directing influence of his Spirit—so he had a twofold end in his death and sufferings: one, the payment of a price of redemption for us to justice; the other, to set before us an example worthy of imitation. Hence his sufferings may be viewed either as satisfactory or as exemplary. Though the sufferings of Christ are proposed* to us as an example, and his death as that which we should imitate by dying for our brethren, at his command;† yet we are not hence to infer that by his death he made no real satisfaction; for the mentioning of the one end does not exclude but supposes the other.

There is a wide difference between a payment made by a debtor in his own person, and a payment made by a surety. As to the reality of payment there is no

* 1 Pet. ii. 21. † 1 John, iii. 16.

difference in the eye of the law, but in relation to grace
there is a striking difference. When a debtor pays
out of his own purse his debts, it cannot be said that
the creditor has forgiven him the debt or shown him
favour ; but if the debt has been paid by another and
that other has been found out by the creditor, then
grace may be said to have been shown. Satisfaction
and remission are inconsistent with each other, when
referred to the same thing, but not so when they are
referred to different things. Satisfaction has God for
its object, remission man for its object. Satisfaction
is made by Christ to God for man, and yet man is
freely pardoned. Justice and mercy kiss each other.
Justice is exercised against sin as imputed to Christ,
and mercy, free and sovereign mercy, is shown to sinners. The pardon granted to us is entirely of grace,
while full satisfaction is demanded of the surety.
Nothing is demanded of us, full payment having been
made by Christ.

If Christ makes satisfaction, we cannot say that he
satisfies himself, in the same character in which he
makes the satisfaction ; he satisfies himself as God and
the Son of God, not as Christ. Thus it is not precisely
in the same character nor in the same relation, that he
gives and receives the satisfaction. Christ gives it
as God-man, as mediator, and receives it as God the
judge. It is indeed absurd to suppose that the same
person should make satisfaction to himself, when the

subject treated of is of a private nature, by which a private loss is compensated or money that is due paid, for in that case the person would take of his own and with it pay himself. But when we speak of a public satisfaction, by which a public injury is repaired, it is not absurd to say that a judge who has violated the law, may make satisfaction to himself as judge by suffering, either in his own person or in the person of another, that punishment which the law denounces; and thus it is in the work of Redemption.

Christ did not suffer eternal death but a death of three days only, and yet he fully paid the debt of everlasting punishment which we owed. His, which was one of finite duration, was equivalent to an everlasting death suffered by us, because of the infinite dignity of his person. His were the sufferings not of a mere man, but of the true God, who purchased the Church with his blood.* Hence what was deficient in duration is supplied by the divinity of the sufferer, which gave infinite importance to a temporary passion. Yet we may not hence infer, that as the person suffering was infinite, one drop of his blood was sufficient for our redemption. The smallest passion of Christ might have infinite value considered merely in relation to the infinite exaltation of him who suffered; yet death only could possess infinite value, in respect of the judge by

* Acts xx. 28.

whose sentence it was inflicted. The dignity of the person increases the dignity of the punishment endured—the more exalted the person is, so much the heavier is the suffering which he undergoes ; yet nothing but that species of punishment which the law denounces can satisfy its claims upon the guilty. Death and death alone could fulfil the demands of law and justice.

It was not necessary, when Christ was suffering the punishment due to sin, that he should suffer that despair and gnashing of teeth, which are a part of the punishment of the damned ; for these are not essential to the punishment which the judge inflicts or which the surety must bear. They are mere circumstances, which arise from the character of the persons of the damned, who, when they find that their torments are overwhelming and eternal, sink into utter despair and gnashing of teeth. This could not be so with Christ, who in the midst of his greatest agonies, had full assurance of deliverance and a resurrection from the tomb, and hence when encompassed by tortures the most excruciating, always manifested his faith in God—" *My* God! *My* God!" are his words.

Though a death of infinite value was due for every individual sinner, yet such a death as Christ's is quite sufficient for the redemption of the whole elect world. A penal satisfaction is not of the same nature with a pecuniary payment, which is valued only by the amount paid, without regard to the person who pays: and hence can be of avail to none but the individual for whom the payment is made. But penal satisfaction is estimated by the dignity of the person who makes it, and is increased in worth in proportion to his dignity, and hence avails for many as well as for one. Money paid by a king is indeed of no more avail in the discharge of a debt, than money paid by a slave: but the life of a king is of more value than the life of a vile slave, as the life of King David was thought of more worth than that of half the Israelitish army.* In this way Christ alone is more excellent than all men together. The dignity of an infinite person swallows up all the infinities of punishment due to us: they sink into it and are lost. Besides, it is no new thing that what is necessary for one should be amply sufficient for many. One sun is necessary to the illumination of an individual, and yet the same sun illuminates the whole human family. One victim was sufficient for the priest and all the people, and yet it would have been requisite for one. Although there were as many atonements necessary as there were Israelites, yet the one great annual expiatory sacrifice atoned for the sins of all the people, because it was so offered for the whole congregation as that by divine appointment it availed

* 2 Sam. xviii. 3.

3

for the case of each singly. On this subject the Scriptures are so express, that no one, unless he have the hardihood to contradict the Holy Spirit, can deny it. " *The Lord laid on him the iniquities of us all.*"* *If one died for all.*† " *By one offering of himself he hath forever perfected them that are sanctified.*"‡ What do all these Scriptures teach, unless that one death of Christ is sufficient to make a full atonement for all the elect, in the same manner as the disobedience of Adam made many sinners?§ One cannot satisfy for many, when he and they are of the same rank. One plebeian cannot satisfy for many plebeians ; but one prince may satisfy for many plebeians. If this is admitted among creatures who are all finite and mortal, how much more between creatures and the Creator, between whom there is an infinite distance ?

The rule which is laid down in Ezekiel 18 : 20, " *the soul that sinneth, it shall die,*" cannot be understood as absolute and universal, for so all imputation of sin would be barred, which yet the Scriptures teach by many examples. It must be referred to the ordinary dispensations of Providence, and not to an extraordinary dispensation of grace. Or it may relate to a particular providence towards the Jews, to whom the Lord speaks in such a way as to close their mouth,

---

* Isai. liii. 6.   † 2 Cor. v. 14.   ‡ Heb. x. 14.
§ Rom. v. 18, 19.

and prevent them from complaining that they had un-
deservedly suffered punishment on account of the sins
of their fathers ; and not to the general government
of men, in which God declares that he will visit the
iniquities of the fathers upon the children until the
third and fourth generation.*

So far is the doctrine of the atonement from opening a door to impiety and spreading a couch on which
spiritual sloth may repose in security, that it is the
most efficacious means of holiness, and the death of sin
itself, which is, among others, one of the ends that
Christ assigns for his death—" that being dead unto
sin, we may live unto righteousness ; that henceforth
we may no more live unto ourselves, but to him who
died for us and was raised again for our justification."
See the 6th chapter of Romans, for the manner in
which the Apostle Paul reasons on this subject ; also
Titus, ii. 14, and 1 Pet. ii. 24.

* Ex. xx. 5.

CHAPTER III.

𝕺n the 𝕻erfection of the 𝕬tonement.

IN the preceding chapter we reasoned against the
followers of Socinus.   In this chapter we contend for
a doctrine that is denied by the Romanists.   They
indeed pretend to hold the unity and perfection of the
satisfaction of Christ, and often exclaim that great
injustice is done them, when they are charged with
maintaining that " *Christ by his sufferings did not make
a full and complete satisfaction for our sins ;*"* while in

* Bellarmine, Book II. concerning Indulgences, chapter 14.

reality they, in many ways, weaken and overturn this doctrine, by maintaining that it must be confined to sins committed before baptism and to the pollution of sin; but that it does not extend to punishment either temporal or eternal.

In order to ascertain distinctly the question, we observe, that a satisfaction made to God is of a nature different from a satisfaction made to man. Among men, satisfactions are of two kinds. One is private, and is called a reparation ; the other public, and is called canonical, because prescribed by the ancient canons of the Church. Satisfaction of the latter kind is very often demanded by civil and ecclesiastical courts, for the reformation of offenders and the removal of scandals. In treating of the satisfaction made to God, we speak strictly concerning the λυτρον, the price of redemption, by which Christ, as our surety, atoned for our transgressions. This is by Romanists in part ascribed to certain meritorious, expiatory works, by which they pretend to atone for their own sins and for those of others. It is of the atonement for sin and satisfaction to justice, which Christ made, that we are to treat in this chapter. The point in controversy is not whether the satisfaction of Christ bars all human satisfactions, public and canonical, or private, which are imposed upon offenders for their correction, and to remove scandals from the Church. We admit that these were, with propriety, often demanded under the Old Testament dispensation, and may yet be laudably exacted. But we inquire, whether, besides the satisfaction made by Christ, other satisfactions for sin are to be made to God, and should be imposed upon the saints? Here we and our opponents are at issue. They affirm that such additional satisfactions are to be made by the saints themselves; while we maintain that they are not only useless, but contrary to the Scriptures.

The infliction of chastisements on the people of God when they go astray—chastisements which are of a medicinal or corrective character, such as are inflicted upon children in their father's house—forms no part of this controversy. We cheerfully admit that God, for valuable purposes, exercises his people with such wholesome discipline. But does the atonement of Christ exclude penal expiatory sufferings on the part of the saints; sufferings designed, not as proofs of their piety, or to heal their backslidings, but as a satisfaction to avenging justice; not inflicted by God as a father and through parental love, but decreed by God as a judge; sufferings which the law denounces against the wicked? Our adversaries affirm that the atonement does not exclude such sufferings. We maintain that it does. The Church of Rome teaches, that though the satisfaction of Christ is of infinite value, yet that it is not so full and ample, but that various atonements are to be made by believers in their own persons. These, they say, are necessary, if not on account of their guilt and liability to eternal punishment, which they admit are taken away by Christ, yet to save them from temporal punishment. Hear what they say: "If any one shall affirm that, on account of the merits of Christ, there is no necessity that we should make any satisfaction to God, through temporal punishments inflicted by Christ and patiently borne by us, or through punishments enjoined by the priest, not voluntarily undertaken—such as penances, prayers, fastings, alms, and other pious exercises— and shall further say that the new life only is the best penitence, let that man be accursed."*

The Remonstrants,† or Arminians, endeavour not a little to destroy the perfection of the atonement. Though they have not yet been so bold as, with the disciples of Socinus, to reject the atonement entirely, yet they make every effort in their power to diminish its efficacy and fulness. They maintain that the satisfaction of Christ was accepted by God, not on account of its own dignity, but merely through grace; that it was not a real, but a nominal satisfaction. The substance of the doctrine which they teach on this head is, that God forbore to punish after the

* Council of Trent, section 4, cap. 8, canon 13.

† A name given to Arminians, on account of the remonstrance which they presented to the Synod of Dort against the act by which their tenets were condemned.

death of Christ, not because satisfaction had been truly rendered to his justice, but because he was graciously pleased to admit the satisfaction, notwithstanding its imperfection, as altogether sufficient.

The doctrine for which we contend is, that Christ hath so perfectly satisfied divine justice for all our sins, by one offering of himself; and not only for our guilt, but also for both temporal and eternal punishment, that henceforth there are no more propitiatory offerings to be made for sin; and that though, for the promotion of their penitence and sanctification, God often chastises his people, yet no satisfaction is to be made by them either in this or a future state of existence.

Such is the perfection of the atonement, that it corresponds to the justice of God revealed in the Word, to the demands of the law, and to the miseries and necessities of those for whom it was made. Had it been in its own nature deficient, and derived its sufficiency only from God's acceptance of it through mere grace, then the victims under the law might have possessed equal efficacy in making atonement for sin, contrary to Heb. x. 4. Its perfection is derived from its own intrinsic fulness of merit. It is perfect: (1.) In respect to *parts;* because it satisfied all the demands which the law makes upon us, both in relation to the obedience of life and the suffering of death. By enduring the punishments due to us, it has freed us from death and condemnation. And by its meritorious efficacy, it has reconciled God the Father to us and has acquired for us a title to eternal life. (2.) It is perfect in *degree;* for Christ has not only done and suffered all that which the law claims of us, but all this in a full and perfect degree; so that nothing more, in this respect, can possibly be desired. The perfection in degree is derived from the infinite dignity of the person who suffered and the severity of the punishment exacted. (3.) Hence follows the perfection in its *effects.* In respect of God, it has effected an entire reconciliation with him;* in relation to sin, it has wrought full expiation and pardon;† and in relation to believers, its effects are perfection in holiness and complete redemption, both as to deliverance from death, and as to a title to life and its possession.‡

We now offer the proofs which establish this view of the atonement.

I. The *dignity of Christ's person*, which is not only of immaculate purity, but also truly divine; a person in which all fulness dwells.§ In Christ's person there is a fulness of divinity, a fulness of office, a fulness of merit and graces. Who, then, can doubt

* Rom. v. 10, and 2 Cor. v. 18.
† Eph. i. 7. Heb. i. 3, and ix. 26.
‡ Heb. ix. 12, and x. 14.   § Col. i. 19.
3*

but that the satisfaction which he has made is one of infinite value and efficacy, and therefore of such fulness and all-sufficiency, that nothing can be added to it? For though Christ's human nature, which was the instrument in the obedience and sufferings, was finite, yet this does not lessen the value of the satisfaction, because it derives its perfection from the divine person of Christ, to which all his actions must be attributed; as he is the person who obeyed and suffered.

II. Our view is also established by *the Oneness of Christ's Offering*. Why does the Apostle Paul assert that Christ has *once* offered himself for us,* and that by one offering of himself he hath forever perfected them that are sanctified? Why does he always set before us the obedience of Christ alone as the ground of our justification, unless this obedience is full and complete? As a repetition of the same offering argues its imperfection, so, on the other hand, an offering's having been but once made, necessarily imports its plenitude and the full accomplishment of its object.

III. The Perfection of the Atonement is confirmed by *the Approbation of God as Judge*. If God declares

---

* Heb. vii. 9 and 10.

that he is perfectly satisfied, let no one dare to say that the satisfaction is imperfect. The question is, whether the supreme judge, who demands the satisfaction, approves of and receives it as altogether sufficient. That the atonement has been approved and accepted by God, is established, not only by the appointment of Christ to the mediatorial office, of whom the Father often declares that he is his beloved Son, in whom he is well pleased; but especially by his resurrection from the dead, which is irresistible evidence both of his divinity and of the perfection of the atonement.* Unless Christ had satisfied to the uttermost, can we believe that God the judge, whose inexorable justice demands full payment, would have freed him, and have exalted him to that supreme glory, which was the reward of his sufferings?† Would the creditor free the surety from prison before he had paid the full debt? Could Christ, when he had undertaken to pay to divine justice the debts which man owed, be set free, until he had to the full redeemed the debt? Seeing, then, that Christ has gloriously arisen, being raised by the power of the Father, there is no room left for doubt respecting the perfection of the satisfaction, the full payment of the price of redemption; of the full discharge of which, the Father has given us such indubitable testimony.

* Rom. i. 4.　　　　　　　　　　　† Phil. ii. 9.

IV. The *effects* which are produced by the atonement prove its entire sufficiency. Why are our reconciliation with God and the appeasing of his wrath; the expiation and pardon of sin, and this not partial, but full and complete; and our redemption and glorification, all attributed to the death and obedience of Christ,* unless his atonement was full and complete? A perfect effect requires a perfect cause to produce it.

The doctrine thus established overthrows at once the Romanist dogmas of the sacrifice of the Mass, of human merits in this life and of Purgatorial expiations hereafter. For if these are allowed, it follows either that Christ's satisfaction is inadequate, or else that God unjustly exacts a double satisfaction for the same sins.

In vain do our opponents contend, " that by pleading for satisfactions to be made by the saints, they do not derogate from the infinity of Christ, nor from his satisfaction; since they make all their virtue and efficacy to depend upon the atonement of Christ, who not only has satisfied for us, but also gives us the power to satisfy for ourselves; and since they do not esteem our good works as atonements to be associated with that of Christ, and as of the same exalted nature, but

---

* See Col. i. 20; 2 Cor. v. 21; 1 John, i. 7; Rom. iii. 24, and v. 10; Heb. i. 3, and ix. 14, and x. 14.

inferior and subordinate." They assume what they
ought to prove. We do not grant that Christ gives
us any power to atone for ourselves. Such a supposition receives no countenance from Scripture, and is
contrary to the very nature of an atonement. It
is one thing to make satisfaction, another to give
the power to make satisfaction. They are indeed
utterly inconsistent with each other. If Christ has
made a complete satisfaction, why is any other demanded? Where the primary cause is solitary, no
co-operative or subordinate causes are admissible. So
far is this doctrine of our opponents from advancing
the glory of Christ, that it in reality, by resorting to
other grounds of salvation than those afforded by him,
offers an indignity to him and his atonement. What
he, as our Redeemer, has engaged to accomplish, they
pretend to effect, at least in part, by other agents.
And though in the application of this redemption, men
are bound to contribute by their efforts as fellow-
workers with God, yet they are unable to co-operate
with him in its acquisition.

Equally futile is their reasoning, when they resort
to the " distinction between sin and punishment, con-
tending that though Christ has satisfied for our sin, he
has not fully satisfied for our punishment; or if for
eternal punishment, at least not for temporal, which
must be suffered by the saints themselves, either in the
present or a future state." Because the remission of

sin on account of the satisfaction made by Christ is perfectly complete; "*there is no condemnation to them who are in Christ Jesus;*" and in consequence of his atonement, their justification is perfect, and in due time they shall obtain full glorification.* Besides, the distinction thus made between sin and its punishment is absurd, for there is a necessary connection between sin and suffering. Sin is the cause and suffering the effect; take away the cause, and the effect is necessarily destroyed. Remission of sin is nothing but a deliverance from all punishment, which cannot be justly inflicted where there is no transgression. Would it be just to demand the payment of a debt which is already either paid or remitted?

They also assert, "that Christ, in a limited sense, makes satisfaction for temporal punishment, in and by us." 1. This assertion is rash, having no countenance from Scripture. 2. It is dangerous, associating men with Christ in making satisfaction, and thus taking a part of the work of redemption out of his hands; for redemption and satisfaction are words of similar import, there being no other way to redeem, but by rendering satisfaction. 3. It is false and contrary to Scripture, which asserts, that Christ by himself hath satisfied once for sin, and that there is no further satisfaction to be made by others.

* Rom. viii. 9.

The view which we have given of the perfection of the atonement prostrates the Arminian doctrine of nominal atonement. When a full payment is made, there is no room for the exercise of grace in accepting what was no more than nominal. In making payments grace is not considered, nor merely the dignity of him who pays, but also the value of the thing given, or its equality to the debt. This is confirmed from Rom. viii. 3, where Christ is said to have been sent, that all righteousness might be fulfilled. Christ fulfilled all righteousness, or satisfied all the demands of the law, by doing what we ourselves were not able to do, on account of the weakness of the law. Now if, by the satisfaction of Christ, the demands of the law are fulfilled in us, this satisfaction must equal the claims of the law. Farther, an imperfect atonement graciously accepted, we cannot admit, for Christ took upon himself* all the punishment which was due to us, even that which was the most grievous, the curse of the law itself.† Finally, if God might have accepted of any imperfect satisfaction, it was unnecessary that Christ should stand as our surety, and be exposed to extreme tortures and a most painful death; for satisfaction could have been received from any other man.

We shall now proceed to remove objections. An

* Isa. liii. 6, 7, 8. † Gal. iii. 13.

objection is drawn from those expressions of Scripture, where the apostles are said to suffer for the Church. But it is one thing to suffer for the Church, in order to purchase her by paying a price of redemption, and another to suffer persecution and death for the purpose of consoling and confirming the people of God, by placing before them an example of patience and obedience. When Paul says that he suffers for the Church or for the body of Christ,* it is not in the former sense, for he elsewhere denies that any one except Christ alone is crucified for us;† but in the latter, as he himself teaches us, 2 Cor. v. 6, *"for your consolation."* In 2 Tim. ii. 10, he says that he endures all things for the elect's sake, not to redeem them from temporal punishment, but that, confirmed and animated by his example, they may obtain salvation by Christ. The remark made by Thomas‡ on this subject is a correct one. *"The sufferings of the saints are profitable to the Church, not as a price of redemption, but as affording it example and exhortation not to depart from the truth."*

When Paul says,§ *" that he fills up that which is behind of the sufferings of Christ,"* he means not the sufferings endured by Christ in his own person; but the sufferings of Christ mystical, i. e., of his body, the Church; sufferings which are to be endured by every

---

* Col. i. 24.   † 1 Cor. i. 13.
‡ 3 Quest. 48, Art. 3.   § Col. i. 24.

Christian, after the manner of Christ, whose members they are. Paul, as well as all other saints, had to take up his cross and follow Christ, and endure that share of tribulation which God allotted him, while on the way to the kingdom of heaven. In filling up this measure of tribulation, the apostle bears his cross with alacrity. Christ is often thus, by a figure, put for his body, the Church: *"Saul, Saul, why persecutest thou me?"** The sufferings of the saints are often called the sufferings of Christ: *"For as the sufferings of Christ abound in us."*† They are called so in relation to their origin, because Christ, as supreme director of the theatre of life, appoints them to us, and calls upon us to suffer them;‡ in relation to their object, for they are laid upon us on account of Christ and his Gospel; and also in relation to our union and communion with Christ, for we are one with him; so that blessings and sufferings are in some sense common to us and Christ: *"In all their afflictions he was afflicted."* We are called to participate in his sufferings, that we may be conformed to him in his cross, before we are conformed to him in his glory.§

It is one thing for a person to atone for his sins by a real satisfaction, another to break them off by works of repentance and charity. It is in the latter sense

---

* Acts ix. 4, and 1 Cor. xii. 12. † 2 Cor. i. 5.
‡ Acts ix. 16; 1 Pet. ii. 21; Phil. i. 29. § Rom. viii. 18.

that Daniel* advises Nebuchadnezzar to break off his sins. The Hebrew word פרק, used by the prophet here, does not primarily signify to redeem, nor even to deliver; its primary sense is to tear away, or break off; and hence, as a collateral signification, to deliver. The prophet exhorts the king to repentance and a change of life, in order to make reparation to men, and not to God, for the injuries and oppressions which he had practised; and that thus, by breaking off his course of sinning, he might be more prosperous, escape from the ruin which was hanging over him, and obtain a longer continuance of peace in his empire. To the same purpose are all those places of Scripture in which pardon of sin is promised to repentance. The repentance is not a meritorious cause, but a condition annexed, the medium through which pardon is obtained.

Sufferings are of two kinds. In the one, they are exacted by a judge to make satisfaction to justice; in the other, they are inflicted for the correction of the offender. We admit that the latter species of offering is often appointed to believers, not for vengeance, but for healing; not for destruction, but for correction. God lays it upon them, not as a judge, but as a father; not out of hatred, but out of love. Cyprian says, *"The Lord chastises the saints that he may advance*

* Dan. iv. 27.

their holiness, and he advances their holiness that he may save them." To the same purpose Thomas speaks:* *"Before pardon, the sufferings of the elect are punishments for sin; after pardon, they are exercises."* Augustin happily explains the difference between the punishments of the wicked and the chastisements of the saints: "All, both good and evil, suffer the same afflictions; nor by their afflictions can we distinguish between the righteous and the wicked; for all things happen alike to all: there is one lot to the righteous and to the wicked. There is, however, a distinction between the persons who suffer. All who are subjected to the same pains are not alike vicious or virtuous. In the same fire gold shines and stubble smokes; by the same fan the chaff is blown away and the wheat purged. Dregs must not be confounded with oil, because both are pressed in the same press. The very same afflictions which prove, purify, and refine the righteous, are a curse and destruction to the wicked. Hence, under the pressure of the same calamities, the wicked detest and blaspheme God, while the righteous pray to him and praise him. Thus the difference is not in the nature of the punishments, but in the character of those who suffer them."†

The chastisements which the saints experience sometimes, indeed, retain the name punishments, but

---

* III. Q. 96.   † De Civ. Dei., lib. i. cap. 8.

not in a strict sense. 1. Because punishments, in a strict sense, are inflicted by the Supreme Judge upon transgressors, on account of their violation of his law. Hence, even after the state of a man is changed and he becomes a saint, the pains and griefs which he suffers are called by the same name, because, though not formally, they are materially the same. 2. Because there are many points of resemblance between them and punishments properly so called: like them, they are not joyous, but grievous to the flesh, which they are designed to subdue; they are dispensed to the saints, by the will of a gracious God, with as much care and attention as he, in the character of an avenging judge, dispenses punishments: sin gives occasion to both: both produce in the mind the same apprehension that God is an angry judge: and both serve as an example salutary to other offenders. But this grand difference still remains—that, in the punishments of the wicked, God, as a judge, has in view satisfaction to his justice; while in the chastisements of his people, he, as a father, designs the correction and amendment of his disobedient children.

The death of David's child, which affliction happened to him after the pardon of his sin,* was not a judicial punishment, but a fatherly chastisement; for his sin having been once pardoned, no punishment

---

* 2 Sam. xii. 14.

could remain to be borne. The reason which God assigns for thus afflicting the King of Israel gives no countenance to the idea that the affliction was judicial and expiatory. By his sin, he had given occasion to the enemy to blaspheme the name of God, and thus the discipline of the house of God had been most basely violated. This breach of discipline must be healed by a salutary example. Nor can we infer that it was judicial, from David's deprecating it. It is the part of human nature to endeavour to escape whatever is painful, just as a sick man deprecates the caustic powders, the pain of the amputating knife, and the bitterness of medicine; though nothing can be further from the nature of punishment than these.

Though death cannot be inflicted upon us to guard us against future transgression, nor for our amendment, yet it by no means follows that it is designed as an atonement for sin. There are many other weighty reasons, rendering it necessary that all should die: such as, that the remains of sin may be destroyed; that we may pass from a natural and terrestrial state to one spiritual and heavenly; that piety may be exercised; that Christian virtues may be displayed in the most brilliant manner; and finally, that we may have a most powerful excitement to amend our life, and prepare for entering upon a better inheritance.

The judgment, which, the Apostle Peter tells us,

must begin at the house of God,* is not the legal judgment of avenging justice, which proceeds from God as a wrathful judge, but a fatherly and evangelical chastisement; not to punish and destroy, but to hold out a useful example, and to correct us, that thus we may not be condemned with the world, as Paul says, (1 Cor. xi. 32.) The *revenge* mentioned 2 Cor. vii. 11, is not properly a punishment inflicted by God in the character of judge; but either an ecclesiastical censure, such as excommunication, which is adjudged by the Church for the removal of scandal; or it rather denotes the repentance and contrition in which a sinner is offended with himself, and, as it were, takes vengeance on himself for his offences.

Though those under the Old Testament dispensation, whose sins were pardoned, had still to offer sacrifices for sin, yet a warrant for attempting to make human atonements is not thence to be inferred. The sacrifices then offered were not, properly speaking, a satisfaction for sin; they were types of a future atonement to be made by Christ, through the efficacy of which they procured pardon.

When Solomon says,† that "*by mercy and truth iniquity is purged,*" no countenance is given to the human satisfaction for which the Church of Rome contends. There are two opinions maintained re-

---

* 1 Pet. iv. 17.   † Prov. xvi. 6.

specting this passage. One is, that by "*mercy and truth*" are meant, the mercy and truth of God: then the wise man would directly allude to and assert the atonement of Christ. The other opinion is, that the mercy and truth of man are intended: then the doctrine which the text teaches would be, that mercy and truth are a condition always required when sin is pardoned, (but not the cause for which the sentence of pardon is pronounced:) because, against the unmerciful, judgment without mercy will be exercised; while on the other hand, "*the merciful shall obtain mercy.*"*

The Hebrew word כפר, which is here translated "purged," does not properly signify expiatory purging, but either covering and remission only, which God bestows on the believing and merciful; or else the removal of the power of sin, in which sense it is used by the Prophet Isaiah.† Then the passage would intimate that the exercise of mercy and sincere piety removes the contrary vices. The following clause of the verse confirms this interpretation of the word: "*By the fear of the Lord men depart from evil.*"

Though nothing defiled can enter into the New Jerusalem, yet there is no need of any satisfaction in this life, besides that of Christ, nor of a purgatory

* Matt. v. 6.   † Isa. xxviii. 18.

in another, to purge away the pollutions of sin; for in the moment of death, when the soul is separated from the body, all the remains of sin are entirely removed by the Spirit of Christ.

CHAPTER IV.

On the Matter of the Atonement.

CONCERNING the matter and parts of the satisfaction, various opinions have been embraced by divines. Some limit it to the sufferings and punishments which he endured for us. This opinion appears to have been first maintained by Cargius, a Lutheran minis-

4

ter, and after him by Piscator, a Reformed professor at Herborne. Some of the divines who embrace it, confine that righteousness by which we are justified to the death which he suffered; while others of them comprehend in it, also, all the sufferings of his life. This they call his passive righteousness. The obedience which he yielded to the precepts of the law, they term his active righteousness, which they suppose to have been necessary in the person of the Mediator to the performance of his mediatorial functions. They maintain, however, that it forms no part of his atonement, or his merits, which are imputed to us.

The common opinion in our churches is, that the atonement made by Christ, which is imputed to us for righteousness before God, is not confined to the sufferings which he endured either in his life or at his death, but extends also to the obedience of his whole life; to all those just and holy actions by which he perfectly obeyed the law in our stead. From these two parts, his sufferings and his obedience, they maintain that the full and perfect price of our redemption proceeds.

In order to ascertain precisely the state of the question, we remark, that the subject of controversy is not, whether Christ perfectly fulfilled both the general law binding him to serve God, and the special law commanding him to submit to death. Nor, whether the obedience of Christ's whole life was for the promotion of our interests, and necessary to procure our salvation. Both are granted by our opponents. They acknowledge that he fulfilled both laws, that the obedience of his life was necessary for him in the performance of his mediatorial duties, and in many respects profitable for us. We inquire whether this obedience forms a part of the satisfaction which he made to God for us; whether it was yielded in our stead.

Again, the inquiry is not, whether the mere sufferings belong to the satisfaction. For those, whose opinion we controvert, acknowledge that no suffering can be of an atoning nature, unless it be of an active character, voluntarily endured. They also admit that, in order to its being acceptable to God, it must include an active obedience or voluntary oblation, which unites the highest love with the most perfect righteousness and holiness. They even say that the observance of the whole law was condensed into one action, that of Christ's death.

But the inquiry is, whether the obedience which Christ through his life yielded to the law, is to be joined to the obedience which he yielded in his death and sufferings, in order to constitute our justifying righteousness before God. We must distinguish between what Christ did directly and immediately to make an atonement, and what only pertained as pre-

vious conditions to his making it. In this last we place
the personal holiness of Christ. Hence the question
is reduced to this point: is the atonement which Christ
made for us restricted to his death alone, or at least
to all those sufferings which were either antecedent
to his death or accompanied it? Or does it comprehend all which Christ did and suffered for us, from the
beginning to the end of his life? The former is the
opinion of Cargius, Piscator, and their followers ; the
latter is our opinion and that of our churches generally. In order to set forth more clearly the doctrine for which we contend, we make the following
remarks:

1. The atoning sufferings of Christ extend to *all*
those which were inflicted upon him, not only in the gar-
den of Gethsemane, but also during his whole life. We
cannot approve of the hypothesis, which restricts the
expiatory sufferings of our Redeemer to the pains he
suffered during the three hours in which the sun was
darkened, and he hung on the cross before his death ;
while it excludes all the other sufferings of his life, as,
at most, necessary only to vindicate the truth of God,
and to accomplish the typical representations of Christ
under the law. We admit, indeed, that the greatest
agonies of Christ were those to which he was exposed
during those hours of darkness. But it is abundantly
evident that all his other sufferings were expiatory.
(1.) Because the Scripture nowhere restricts his expia-

tion to the three hours in which the sun was darkened, but refers it to his sufferings in general, without
any limitation.* They even extend it to his whole
humiliation.† (2.) Because the agonies which he endured in the garden, and which are expressed by the
words *grief, sorrow, agony, heaviness, amazement,* and
being exceeding sorrowful even unto death, on account of
the tremendous weight of divine wrath and malediction, were the chief sufferings which Christ had to
endure in his soul for us. (3.) The contrary opinion
wrests from many pious Christians one great means of
consolation. In the sufferings of Christ's whole life,
as expiatory, they find rest to their souls. This idle
imagination of Cargius and Piscator would snatch
from Christians all this solace, and deprive them of
innumerable evidences of the divine love.

The objection which is brought against this reasoning from Zech. iii. 9: " *I will remove the iniquity of
that land in one day,*" is of no avail. That from these
words of the Apostle, "*We are sanctified through the offering of the body of Jesus once for all,*"‡ is equally unsubstantial. The inference to be drawn from these texts
is not that the sufferings of Christ, antecedent to those
on the cross, are not expiatory; but only that the atonement was consummated on the cross. In consequence

* Isa. liii. 4, 5. 1 Pet. ii. 21, and iii. 18. Matt. xvi. 21. Heb. v. 7,
and x. 8, 9.   † Phil. ii. 6, 7.   ‡ Heb. x. 10.

of this consummation all the sins of all the elect were, in one day, blotted out.   The reason why the Apostle, by a figure common in all languages, refers the expiation of our sins to the one offering of Christ, is, that his sufferings on the cross were the last and most piercing, without which all his antecedent sufferings would have been insufficient; as the payment of the last farthing completes the liquidation of the debt and cancels the bond.   Because he was inaugurated into his mediatorial office, in the thirtieth year of his age, we may not thence infer, that previously to that time, he was neither a priest nor a victim ; for by the same mode of reasoning, it would follow, that before thirty years of age he was not a Mediator.   That Christ was in favour with God, that he was his well-beloved Son, nay, that he was sometimes in his life glorified, does not prove that he did not then bear the divine wrath. These two are not at all incompatible with each other. Christ, viewed in himself, never ceased to be most dearly beloved of his Father, not even in his excruciating tortures on the accursed tree, though, as our surety, he bore the load of the divine wrath, and was made a curse for us.   It was not necessary that the punishment which Christ underwent should be so intense, that it could admit of no intervals of alleviation by which he might be animated to encounter gloriously the dreadful conflict set before him.

2. In the actions and sufferings of Christ, *two things*

are to be considered: their substance and their form. They are considered in relation to their substance, when we examine their nature and intensity. They are considered formally, when they are examined as constituting a righteousness to be sustained before the tribunal of God. In the former light the actions and sufferings are many and various. In the latter they are to be considered under one form only, that of a whole, composed of all his actions and passions—a one and perfect righteousness. Wherefore one action or passion alone cannot be said to effect a full atonement, because it is necessary that a perfect obedience should be connected with it. Hence, although various degrees and acts may be remarked in the obedience of Christ, which commenced at his birth, was continued through his life, and completed at his death, yet it is unique, as to the completion of the work of salvation and the righteousness which it accomplishes.

3. There is in the obedience of Christ *a twofold efficacy.* The one is expiatory, that by which we are freed from those punishments to which we were liable on account of sin. The other is a meritorious efficacy, by which, through the remission of our sins, a title to eternal life and salvation has been acquired for us. For as sin has brought upon us two evils—the loss of life, and exposure to death ; so redemption must procure two benefits—liberation from death, and a title to life: or, deliverance from hell and an introduction

into heaven.   There are various passages of Scripture which clearly express these two benefits. "*To make reconciliation for iniquity, and to bring in an everlasting righteousness.*"*   "*Christ hath redeemed us from the law, being made a curse for us—that the blessing of Abraham might come on the Gentiles.*"†   "*God sent forth his Son—to redeem them that were under the law, that we might receive the adoption of sons.*"‡   "*We were reconciled to God by the death of his Son; much more being reconciled, we shall be saved by his life.*"§   "*That they may receive forgiveness of sins, and inheritance among them which are sanctified.*"‖

These two blessings, indeed, which flow from the obedience of Christ, are indissolubly connected in the covenant of grace, so that no one who obtains the pardon of sin can fail of acquiring a right to life. Yet they must be distinguished, and not confounded as if they were one and the same thing.   It is one thing to free from death, another to introduce into life ; one thing to deliver from hell, another to conduct into heaven ; one thing to free from punishment, another to bestow rewards.   Though it is true that no one is freed from death, who is not also made a partaker of life, yet it does not follow that a deliverance from the death which we deserve is not to be distinguished

---

* Dan. ix. 24.   † Gal. iii. 13, 14.   ‡ Ibid. iv. 4.
§ Rom. v. 10.   ‖ Acts xxvi. 18.

from the acquisition of glory. There are many grades of life as well as of holiness. The possession of life does, indeed, follow liberation from death, but it is not necessary that this life should be a happy and glorious one ; as liberty follows deliverance from prison, but it may be liberty without a throne and a diadem. Joseph might have been freed from prison and not set over the land of Egypt. Between death and life simply there is no medium, but between eternal death, and a life happy and glorious, there is a medium—the life of bondage in which man is now placed. The present life, in which man is bound to the performance of duty, is a state of pilgrimage, not of heavenly rest.

While we believe it necessary to make distinctions such as these, we think it improper to inquire curiously, as some do, by what particular acts Christ made atonement, and by what he merited life for us. Those who make these too nice distinctions, attribute the atonement to his sufferings ; and the acquisition of a right to life, to his active obedience to the law. These distinctions receive no countenance from Scripture, which nowhere distinguishes the obedience of Christ into parts, but, on the contrary, represents it as a thing unique, by which he hath done in our place everything which the law requires of us. As Christ, by the obedience of his life, has rendered to the law that which it required of us, and to which we were

4*

otherwise personally bound ; so by this obedience he has satisfied the law, as to those demands which it makes upon us : and hence his active obedience partakes of the nature of satisfaction. Again, as his passive obedience proceeded from unspeakable love to us, and as love is the fulfilling of the law, we cannot deny but it was meritorious, and of the nature of a price of redemption, by which a right to life has been acquired for us. Therefore, we should avoid those curious distinctions, and consider liberation from death and our right to life as flowing from all the mediatorial duties, which Christ performed during his humiliation, and which, considered as a whole, are called the obedience of Christ. Sin could not be expiated before the law was fulfilled, nor could a right to life be acquired, before the charges preferred against us on account of sin were blotted out. Christ merited by making atonement, and by meriting he made atonement.

Herein lay the utmost merit that he performed a most arduous work, impossible to all other beings and by no means obligatory upon himself, by his perfect obedience. This obedience was at once a great proof of love to us, an act of submission to the Father and a conformity to the special law of his own vocation. Yet it would have been of no avail to us, had it not been sealed and consummated by his death. The atonement is not to be ascribed merely to the external shedding of his blood, but also, and principally, to an internal act—his spontaneous and unchangeable will to suffer even to the death of the cross for us. By this voluntary offering of himself, we are said to be sanctified.* It is to be ascribed to the payment not of the last farthing, but of the whole of the price of redemption, which is Christ, delivering up and subjecting himself for us.

The objection which Socinus offers against this is of no force. He says, that "atonement and merit are incompatible with each other, for satisfaction or atonement is the payment of a just debt, whereas merit is effected by giving something not due on the score of justice." This is accurate when applied to a satisfaction or payment made by a debtor in his own person, but not when applied to a vicarious satisfaction, in which a surety, while making satisfaction, may have merit with both the debtor and the creditor : with the debtor, by paying, when under no obligation to do so, a debt for him, and thus graciously freeing him from all obligation to the creditor : with the creditor also, especially if a covenant has been made, in which it is stipulated that upon making a specified payment, it shall be admitted not only as a satisfaction for sin, but as procuring a title to blessings not otherwise due. This is the case here, as appears from Isa. liii. 10; Heb. ix. 15; Col. i. 19, 20, and similar passages.

* Heb. x. 14.

4. There are two things contained in the law. These are *precepts*, which prescribe duties; and *sanctions*, which ordain rewards to those who keep the law, and punishments to its transgressors. Man, who is under the obligation of the law, may be at the same time bound both to obedience and punishment. This, however, cannot take place in a state of primitive rectitude, but in a state of sin. For sinful man sustains a twofold relation to God—one the relation of a creature, the other that of a sinful and condemned creature. In the former he always owes obedience to God, and can never be freed from this obligation so long as he continues a creature, no matter how situated. In the latter he is obnoxious to punishment. Yet we cannot infer from this doctrine that man pays his debt twice to God. A penal debt is very different from a debt of obedience. A penal debt arises from past transgressions ; a debt of obedience, from the indispensable obligation of the creature to obey the Creator, which is coextensive with the whole term of its existence, and neither is nor can be relaxed, even while the creature is suffering the punishment of its transgressions.

5. There is a *threefold subjection* to the law—a natural, a federal, and a penal subjection. The natural subjection arises from the law as a rule of holiness, and respects the creature as a creature. It is eternal and indispensable, because, in every situation, the crea-

ture is bound to be subject to God and to obey him. The federal subjection arises from the law as prescribing a condition, upon the fulfilment of which a reward is to be attained; respects the creature as placed in a covenant state; and prescribes the performance of duty under the promise of rewards and punishments. The penal subjection respects the creature as placed in a state of sin and condemnation, and binds him to suffer the punishment which the law denounces. The first is absolute and immutable; for as long as there is a creature and a Creator, the creature must be subject to the Creator. God can no more dispense with his claim of subjection upon the creature than he can deny himself. The second is economical and changeable, because, as it respects man not in a natural, but in a constituted state, it continues in force as long as man continues in that state, and no longer. So soon as he has finished his probation, and, by fulfilling the condition, has obtained the reward, he is freed from his subjection. The third is necessary and inevitable, whenever the creature falls into sin, which is always followed by punishment. The first is founded in a right essential to God; in his natural, underived, and necessary authority over the creature, and in the natural dependence of the creature upon him. The second is founded in the sovereign pleasure of God, whereby he has been pleased to enter into a covenant with his creature, and promise life under this or that condition. The third is founded in the judicial authority and vindicatory justice of God, by which he avenges the transgressions of his creature. "Vengeance is mine, and I will repay." All creatures, angels and men, are under the natural subjection to the law. Adam, in a state of innocence, was under the federal subjection. Devils and reprobate men are under the penal subjection.

In this third respect, it is easy to conceive how Christ was subjected to the law—"*Made under the law*," as the apostle expresses it; and whether he was subjected to the law for himself or for us. As a man, there is no doubt but he was subject to the law for himself as a rule of holiness,* by a common and natural subjection, under which angels and glorified saints are in heaven, who are bound to love and serve God. But it does not follow from this that he was subject to the

---

* Witsius, the elegant author of the "Economy of the Covenants," as well as Turrettin and President Edwards, takes this view of the obligations of Christ as a creature. But, as Turrettin says the human nature of Christ is only an adjunct of his divine person, he could owe no obedience for himself. It is a person only, who is the subject of the moral law, and the person of Christ is the second person of the Trinity, who is Lord of the law. His humility is everywhere in Scripture represented as voluntary. Had he been subject to the law for himself, he could not have performed an obedience for others. Those great divines rather express themselves loosely than erroneously; not foreseeing the bad use which men of subtle and unsound mind would make of their inaccurate phrases.

law as to that which imposed the indispensable conditions of happiness. Nor that he was federally subject to it, so as to need to earn eternal life by obedience, for such life was his already by virtue of the hypostatical union. Much less was he bound by a penal subjection, for he was most holy and absolutely free from all sin. So that when he undertook the twofold office of fulfilling the precepts of the law, and suffering its sanction, all this was to be done in consequence of a voluntary arrangement, by which he, as Mediator, engaged to perform them for us. It resulted from his covenant with his Father, to do and suffer as our surety all those things which the law claimed of us, and which were necessary to our redemption.

These remarks being premised in order to an accurate understanding of the subject, we now proceed to offer proofs in support of our opinion. It is confirmed from many passages of Scripture.

I. The first we adduce is Rom. v. 19: *"For as by the disobedience of one many were made sinners; so by the obedience of one, are many made righteous."* Here the atonement is referred to his obedience, not to that of his death, but also that of his life. 1. Because the apostle treats of his whole obedience, without any limitation; hence this obedience must be perfect, and continued from the beginning of his life to the end.

An incomplete obedience will not suit the language here used by the Spirit.   2. He treats concerning an obedience, which imports universal conformity to the law, not only with respect to the penal sanction, but also, and indeed chiefly, with respect to observing its precepts.   3. He treats of what is called, v. 17, the "*gift of righteousness*," which cannot be applied to the sufferings of Christ.   4. He speaks of an obedience which is opposed to the disobedience of Adam; and as the disobedience of Adam was a violation of the whole law, so the obedience of Christ must be a fulfilment of the whole law.   5. Of an obedience which was due from us, both as to precept and penalty.   It will be of no avail to object, " that the obedience is nothing else than the one righteousness mentioned verse 18, and which is said to be to justification of life, and that the condemnation of sin under which we have fallen arose from one sinful act of Adam."   The righteousness spoken of here does not intend one act of righteousness; it denotes a righteousness effected by a complete and perfect obedience.   Nor, though the offence came upon all from one sin, can the righteousness be derived to all from one act: because the least failure in performing the demands of the law is sin; whereas righteousness requires the fulfilment of the whole law.

II. The obedience of Christ is said to have been

*even to death,** in which not only its intensity as to degree is expressed, an intensity the greatest which can be rendered by any one; but also its extension and duration, from the beginning of his life to its end. This appears from his obedience being referred to the whole of his humiliation, which appeared not in his death only, but in his whole life. In other portions of Scripture, the obedience of Christ is described by the writing of the law in his heart,† and his active observance of it.‡ Again, it is spoken of as a race which Christ had to run,§ and as a work which he had to perform.‖ These were not to be consummated by one act, but to be a constant tenor of obedience through his whole life.

III. It behoved Christ to be made in the likeness of sinful flesh, that he 'might *supply* what the law could not do, in that it was *weak*, and fulfil the claims of the law in us.¶ This weakness of the law is not to be understood subjectively, as if it were in the law, but objectively, in the sinner in relation to the law; on account of his inability to perform any one of the duties which it commands. This law is said to be weak, not in relation to the infliction of punishment, but as to the observation of its precepts. Christ, therefore, by

* Phil. ii. 8. † Psal. xl. ‡ Heb. x. 5.
§ Heb. xii. 1, 2. ‖ John xvii. 4. ¶ Rom. viii. 3, 4.

supplying what the law could not do in us, must fulfil
all the law demanded of us, and work out what the
apostle calls " righteousness," or the rights of the law,
without doubt a right to life, obtained by doing what
the law commands. This required not only a passive,
but also an active obedience. For seeing the law and
commands of God are the same, punishments cannot
be said to fulfil the law, or its commands. They
satisfy its denunciations only. Who would say that
a malefactor, who had been capitally punished for his
crimes, had obeyed the king or the law? To act
agreeably to law is a good and praiseworthy thing,
which cannot be asserted respecting the suffering of
punishment, *per se*, unless it will be asserted, that he
is to be applauded who suffers the punishments of
hell.

IV. We argue, in favour of extending the atonement to the active obedience of Christ, from his being
bound to *all* that the law required of us, in order to
acquire a title to life. To this, obedience of life was no
less requisite than the suffering of death; because the
sinful creature is bound to both these, and both were
necessary to the obtaining of pardon and a right to
life. In the law, life is not promised to him who
suffers its penalties, but to him who performs its
duties. " *Do this and thou shalt live.*" Hence, to undergo the penalty by dying, was not sufficient, without

the obeying of the precepts. Let it not here be objected, " that there is a difference between evangelical and
legal justification; that in the latter a perfect obedience to the law is requisite, but not in the former."
The difference of our justification now under the Gospel, from that under the covenant of works, is not
placed in the thing itself, but in the manner in which
we obtain it. Justification, whether legal or evangelical, must be founded on a righteousness, perfect, absolutely perfect, in all its parts; a righteousness which
shall comply with all the conditions that the law imposes for the purpose of obtaining eternal life; a
righteousness which shall answer to the eternal and
immutable claims of God upon the creature. These
were qualities in that righteousness by which we were
to be justified, that could not be dispensed with even
in Christ; " for he came not to destroy the law, but to
fulfil it."*   The only difference of our justification lies
in the manner in which it comes to us. What the law
demanded of us as a perfect righteousness to be
wrought out in our own persons, has been wrought by
another, even by Christ, in our stead.

V. We infer that the active obedience of Christ is
comprehended in that atonement which he made for
sin, from the atonement's being founded in his *right-*

---

* Matt. v. 17, and Rom. iii. 31.

eousness, as appears from various passages of Scripture.*
Whence justification is said† to be effected by the imputation of righteousness. But the righteousness of
Christ does not consist in his suffering, but in his
doing. The righteousness of the law is not obtained
by suffering, but by doing, even as the sentence of condemnation is pronounced for sinning. Christ testifies,
that it " became him to fulfil all righteousness,"‡ by doing in everything the will of his Father; and Paul says,
" that Christ was made sin for us, that we might be made
the righteousness of God in him."§ By which it is to
be understood, that, as those sins which violated the
law were imputed to Christ, so his righteous actions,
by which he fulfilled the law, are imputed to us for a
justifying righteousness.

VI. The same doctrine is established from 1 Cor. i.
13, where it is said, that *Christ is not divided.* Hence,
we infer that his righteousness is not to be divided,
but, as a whole and unique inheritance, is to be bestowed on us. The paschal lamb was to be eaten
whole; and, in like manner, Christ, who was typically
represented by that lamb, is to be received by us in
all his mediatorial fulness, both as to what he did and
what he suffered. This view of the subject attributes

---

* Rom. i. 17, and iii. 21, and v. 18.   Phil. iii. 2.   Dan. ii. 24.
† Rom. iv.   ‡ Matt. xiii. 15.   § 2 Cor. v. 21.

greater glory to Christ and presents richer fountains of consolation. This consolation is greatly diminished by those who take away from the price of our redemption a part of his perfect righteousness and most holy obedience, and thus rend his seamless coat.

We shall now proceed to the removal of objections. If our redemption and salvation are attributed to the death and blood of Christ, this is not done to the exclusion of the obedience of his life; for such a restriction is nowhere mentioned in Scripture. On the contrary, the work of man's salvation is, in many places, as shown above, attributed to the obedience and righteousness of Christ. When the death or blood of Christ is mentioned alone, and our redemption ascribed to it, this is done by a synechdoche, a figure which puts a part for the whole. The reason is, that his death was the lowest degree of his humiliation and the completion of his obedience, that which supposes all the other parts, and without which they would have been of no avail. No righteousness merits anything unless it is persevered in to the last breath; a payment is never perfectly made, until the last farthing is paid and the bond cancelled.

Though the Apostle Paul attributes* the blessedness of the saints to the remission of sin which flows from

* Rom. iv. 7.

the blood of Christ, yet it does not follow from this, that all our righteousness and the whole of the satisfaction made by Christ, are founded in his passion. For the apostle does not argue from the pardon of sin's being precisely equivalent to the imputation of righteousness and its proceeding precisely from the same thing in the atonement; but from the indissoluble connection among the blessings of the new covenant, a connection so intimate, that every one who obtains pardon of sin, necessarily and immediately obtains a right to life and becomes an heir of the kingdom of heaven. In the same way Paul treats of love to our neighbour, and the fulfilling of the whole law, as the same thing;* because, when love to our neighbour exists, all the other duties of the law will necessarily be performed.

Though each obedience of Christ, as well that of his life as of his death, was perfect in its kind, yet neither of them alone was a sufficient satisfaction, which required the observance of precepts as well as the suffering of punishments, that liberation from death and a right to life might be procured. One does not exclude the other; nay, they mutually include each other.

What one person owes for himself, he cannot pay for another, if he be a private person. But nothing prevents such a payment, when the person is a public

* Gal. v. 14.

character, who may act both in his own name and in the name of those whom he represents. He who pays what he owes for himself, cannot by the same thing make a payment for others, unless he has voluntarily made himself a debtor for them, in which case he can. For, although he may be a debtor, yet this character arises from his own voluntary act—the debt which he has to pay for himself is a debt which, were it not for his own voluntary deed, he is not bound to pay, and hence, while he is paying for himself, he may, by the same act, pay for another. So Christ, who became man, not for his own sake, but for our sakes, was under obligation to fulfil the law in order to merit life, not for himself, but for us. Though Christ, as a creature, was naturally subject to the law, yet he was not under it by a covenant and economical subjection, binding him to obtain life for himself, and stand as a surety in the room of sinners; for this arose from a voluntary agreement entered into between him and his Father. In an economical sense, he owed nothing for himself, because he is the Son of God, and Lord of the law. As to his human nature, he was not thus bound either absolutely or partially. Not absolutely, for his human nature was an adjunct of his divine person; and as this was not subject to the law, neither could the nature be which was assumed by it. Moreover, since the assumption of human nature was a part of his humiliation, the same must be true of all that results from that assumption. One of these results is the subjection to the law. Not relatively, because, as man, he was not bound by the old legal covenant, which belonged only to those whom Adam represented, and who were naturally descended from him. From all which I infer, that he had no need to perform the duties of the law to acquire for himself a right to life; which right, of necessity, results from the connection of his human nature with the Logos, the second person of the Trinity. Hence also I infer, that Christ owed all his covenant obedience for us, and this in the character of a surety who represented us.

Though Christ obeyed God in our room, we cannot thence infer that we are no longer bound to obedience in our own persons. It is indeed fairly to be inferred, that we are not bound to obey for the same end and from the same cause—to obtain life by the performance of duties, to which we are bound by covenant obligation. Yet we may be, and are, in perfect consistency with the obedience of Christ for us, bound by a natural obligation to yield the same obedience to God, not that we may obtain life, but because we have obtained it; not that we may acquire a right to heaven, but that, having through Christ obtained a title, we may be prepared for entering upon its enjoyment. Hence, though Christ has died for us, we are still obnoxious to natural death; not, however, for a punishment, but for a deliverance from the evils of this life and an introduction into heaven.

We must distinguish between a righteousness of innocence, which takes place when one is accused of no fault, and a righteousness of perseverance, to which a reward is due for duties done. The pardon of sin produces the former kind of righteousness, by taking away every accusation on account of sins committed; but it does not of necessity so produce the latter, that he who obtains it must be forthwith adjudged to have performed all duties. It is one thing to free a person from the punishment which is due to the omission of duty; another to account him really righteous with the righteousness of perseverance to which life is promised, just as if he had omitted no duty and done no evil. The former of these is obtained in the day of pardon, but not the latter; which would be contrary to truth and the just judgment of God. Pardon does not remove sin, but prevents its imputation. He who is pardoned may and does commit sin; but in consequence of the pardon which he has obtained, it shall not be imputed to him for condemnation. Pardon takes away only the guilt of sin, and consequently its punishment, but not its pollution. Thus, to be viewed as having done no sin and as having omitted no duty, can be understood in a twofold sense: 1. In relation to punishment—that we can no more be punished than if we had in reality

5

committed no sin and omitted no duty; because we
are freed from all that punishment which is due to sin.
2. In relation to the obtaining of reward—that he
who is esteemed to have performed all duty and
avoided all sin, shall be judged by God to have done
all things which are necessary to life. In this latter
sense, it is not true that he whose sins are remitted is
to be esteemed free from all sin; for, as was remarked
above, pardon takes away punishment; but God is
not, by the sentence of pardon which he pronounces,
bound to hold the sinner as free from all delinquency,
as having fulfilled all his duty, and as a perfectly just
person. This is not true in fact. The guilty is not
to be esteemed righteous, because, through supplication and confession, he has obtained pardon from the
Judge.

It cannot be said that God demands a double payment of the same debt. For the law binds the sinner
both to obedience and punishment, as is said above;
and the actions and sufferings of Christ do not constitute a double payment, but both together constitute one payment; one unique righteousness, by which
deliverance from death and a right to life have been
acquired for us.

A perfect fulfilment of the law cannot be said to
have been condensed into the voluntary death of
Christ. For the law demands perfect obedience to
all its several precepts, and this not in degree only,

but in duration, from the beginning to the end of life; all which cannot be accomplished in one action.

So far is the whole of Christ's righteousness, which is imputed to us, from being placed in his sufferings, that, strictly speaking, no righteousness is placed in suffering, but in doing only. No one can be called righteous merely because he suffers, for misery is not virtue. Besides, sufferings yield no obedience to those commands of the law to which life is promised; they only satisfy its sanctions, and cannot be called, *per se*, righteousness. If there is any righteousness in punishment, it belongs to the person who inflicts the punishment, and not to him who is punished.

Calvin, in many parts of his works, teaches the doctrine for which we contend. Take the following passages.* "When it is asked how, by the removal of sin, Christ hath taken away the enmity between God and us; and brought in a righteousness which hath made God our friend? It may be answered in general, that he has done this by the whole course of his obedience. This is proved by the testimony of Paul, *as by the transgression of one, many were made sinners, so by the obedience of one, many were made right-eous.* Elsewhere, the ground of pardon, that which de-livers us from the curse of the law, the same apostle extends to the whole of Christ's life. '*When the ful-*

* Inst., book ii., cap. 16, sec. 5.

*ness of time was come, God sent forth his Son, made under
the law, to redeem them that were under the law.'* Even
in his baptism, God declares, Christ fulfilled a part of
this righteousness, because he obeyed his Father's will.
Finally, from the time that '*he took upon himself the
form of a servant,*' he began to pay the price of our
redemption. Nevertheless, that the Scripture may
define more precisely the manner in which salvation
is procured, it ascribes peculiarly the price of redemption to the death of Christ." He afterwards adds,
" Yet the remaining part of his obedience which he performed during his life is not excluded; for the apostle
comprehends the whole of his obedience from the beginning of his life to the end, when he says, that '*he
humbled himself, and took upon him the form of a servant, and was obedient to his Father unto death, even the
death of the cross.*' Indeed, his death occupies the first
grade in his voluntary subjection; because a sacrifice
availed nothing, unless it was offered freely." Elsewhere, he remarks,* that " accepting grace, is nothing
else but his unmerited goodness, by which the Father
embraces us in Christ, clothes us with his innocence,
causing us to accept it, that on account of it, he may
esteem us holy, pure and innocent. It behooves the
righteousness of Christ, which alone is perfect and
will stand in the sight of God, to be presented for us,

---

* Inst., book iii. cap. 14, sec. 12.

and as a righteousness offered by our surety, to be set to our account in the judgment. Furnished with this, we, through faith, obtain perpetual remission of sin. By its immaculate purity, all our defilements are washed away: they are not laid to our account, but before the splendour of Immanuel's righteousness, are banished and flee away, never more to rise against us in judgment."

The Gallic Synods, by repeated acts, have given their most explicit testimony in favour of the same truth.* "Since man can find in himself, either before or after effectual calling, no righteousness by which he can stand before the tribunal of God, he cannot be justified unless in our Lord Jesus Christ, who was obedient to God the Father, even from his entrance into the world until his ignominious death on the cross. In his life and at his death, he fulfilled the whole law given to man and the command to suffer and lay down his life, a price of redemption for many. By this perfect obedience we are rendered righteous; for through the goodness of God it is imputed to us and received by faith, which is the gift of God. We, by the merit of the whole of this obedience, obtain remission of our sins and are rendered worthy of eternal life."

---

* Privatensis Synodus, anno 1612, and Tonninensis, anno 1614.

CHAPTER V.

On the Extent of the Atonement.

THE controversy concerning the extent or universality of the atonement has been, and still is, greatly agitated, which imposes upon us a necessity of handling it, that nothing may be wanting to a clear elucidation of this all-important article of the Christian system.

Among the ancients, the Pelagians and Semi-Pelagians contended that Christ died for all men; hence Prosper, in his letter to Augustine, concerning the remains of the Pelagian heresy, says, " Those who embrace the Pelagian heresy profess to believe that Christ died for all men universally, and that none are excluded from the atonement and redemption which the blood of Christ has effected." And among those errors which they attribute to Augustine, they find this: " The Saviour was not crucified for the redemption of the whole world." Faustus* says, " They wander far from the path of piety, who assert that Christ did not die for all." Hincmar, in his letter to Pope Nicholas,† recounts it as one of the errors of Gotteschalcus, that he preached that Christ did not shed his blood, precious to God the Father, for the redemption and salvation of all men, but for those only who will be saved, or for the elect. To the same purpose are the anathemas of the pretended Council of Arles, recorded in a letter to Lucidus, written by Faustus, the standard-bearer of the Semi-Pelagians; a Council which Sirmundus does not deny

* Book i., De Libero Arbitrio.
† Flodoardus, book iii., chap. 14.

to have been Semi-Pelagian. Augustine, in his age, opposed himself to these heretical innovations; so did his disciples, Prosper and Fulgentius, and other preachers of the grace of Christ, who, travelling in their footsteps, boldly defended the truth. The same was afterwards asserted by Remigius, bishop of Leyden.[*]

The controversy was afterwards renewed among the Roman Catholics, some of whom taught, like the Semi-Pelagians, the doctrine of universal atonement; while others, embracing the views of Augustine and his genuine disciples, restricted the atonement to the elect. This controversy was principally between the Jesuits and Jansenists. The Jesuits, a genuine branch of the Semi-Pelagian sectaries, warmly contend for a universal atonement. The Jansenists with great firmness contended that the atonement was restricted to the elect. In this they followed Jansenius, the founder of their order, who has examined this subject very largely, and with great solidity of argument.[†]

The controversy passed from the Romanists to the Protestants. The Lutherans follow the Jesuits, and contend for a universal satisfaction.[‡] The Arminians, however, called Remonstrants from the remonstrance

---

[*] Liber de tribus epistolis, et Concilio Valentino III. anno 855 habito.

[†] In suo Augustino, et in Apologia Jansenii, et in Catechismo de Gratia.

[‡] Eckard. Fascicul. controv. c. 15. De Prœdesti. q. 6. Brochmanus de gratia Dei. c. 2, q. 17, 18, 19, et alii.

which they presented to the Synod of Dort, are its great champions. They have indirectly recalled Romanism, and have drawn the most of their errors from Molinus, Lessius, Suarezius, and other Jesuits. From such polluted fountains they have obtained their error concerning universal atonement, which is placed second among those that were rejected and condemned by the Synod of Dort, as may be seen in the second chapter of their "Rejection of Errors concerning the Death of Christ."

The doctrine on this subject for which the Arminians contended at the Synod of Dort, is expressed in this manner:—"The price of redemption which Christ offered to his Father, was not only in itself sufficient for the redemption of the whole human family, but even by the decree, will and grace of God the Father, was paid for all men and every man, so that no one is, by an antecedent decree of God, particularly excluded from a participation of its fruits. Christ, by the merits of his death, has so far reconciled God to the whole human family, that the Father on account of his merits, without any impeachment of his truth or justice, can enter and wishes to enter into and confirm a new covenant of grace with sinful men exposed to damnation." 1. Hence they maintain, that according to the counsel of God, Christ so died for all men that not only is his death, on account of its own intrinsic value, sufficient for the redemption of all men, but that

5*

agreeably to the will of God it was offered for that express purpose: that it was a death in the room of all men and for their good, by the intervention of which, God ever after willed to deal graciously with all men; and hence, that the death of Christ was not a blessing promised in the covenant of grace, but the very foundation of it. 2. That by his own intention and that of his Father, he has obtained for all men, as well those who perish as those who are saved, a restoration into a state of grace and salvation, so that no one, on account of original sin, is either exposed to condemnation or will be condemned; but all are freed from the guilt of that sin. 3. That Christ, according to the counsel of his Father, delivered himself up to death for all men, without any fixed purpose that any individual in particular should be saved; so that the necessity and utility of the atonement made by the death of Christ might be in every respect preserved, although the redemption obtained should not be actually applied to one individual of the human family. 4. That Christ by his atonement merited faith and salvation for none, with such certainty, that the atonement must be applied to them for salvation; but merely acquired for God the Father a perfect will and power to treat with man upon a new footing, to enter into a covenant either of grace or of works with man, and to prescribe whatever conditions he chose; the performance of which conditions depends entirely on the free will of man, so that it became possible that either all or none should fulfil them. 5. That the procurement of salvation is more extensive than its application; as salvation was obtained for all but will be applied to very few. All these are clearly proved to be Arminian tenets, from the *Collation* published at the Hague, and from the *exposé* of their sentiments in their remonstrance against the second article of the Synod of Dort.

Those of our ministers, who defend the doctrine of universal grace, give great countenance to not a few of these Arminian tenets, nay, in a great measure adopt them as their own. That they may evince a philanthropy, a love of God towards the whole human family, they maintain that Christ was sent into the world by the Father as a universal remedy, to procure salvation for all men under the condition of faith. They say that though the fruit and efficacy of Christ's death will be enjoyed by a few only, on whom God, by a special decree, has determined to bestow them, yet Christ died with an intention to save all, provided they would believe:* In this manner, they teach that the decree of the death of Christ preceded the decree of election, that in sending Christ into the world, no special respect was had to the elect any more than to the rep-

---

* The opinion here unfolded is, with very little variation, that of the Hopkinsians.—*Translator.*

robate, and that Christ was appointed to be equally the Saviour of all men. They even distinctly assert that salvation was not intended to be procured for any particular persons, but the possibility of salvation for all. This, they tell us, was effected by the removal of obstacles which justice placed in the way of man's salvation, which was done by rendering satisfaction to justice and thus opening a door of salvation, that God reconciled by the atonement might, in consistency with the claims of justice, think of entering into a new covenant with man and of bestowing upon him salvation. But as God foresaw that on account of the wickedness of their hearts, none would believe in Christ, he, by another special decree, determined to bestow upon some faith, thus enabling them to accept of salvation and become partakers of it; while the rest of the human family would remain in unbelief, and on its account would be justly condemned. In this they differ from the Arminians, and embrace in so far the truth of the atonement. Such views as these which we have stated are clearly contained in their writings. Camerus* says, " The death of Christ, under the condition of faith, belongs equally to all men." Testardus:† " The end of giving Christ for a propitiation in his blood was, that a new covenant might be entered into with the whole human family, and that, without

---

* In Cap. 2, Epist. ad Heb. ver. 9.   † In Ireni. The. 78, et 79.

any impeachment of justice, their salvation might be rendered possible, and an offer of it made to them in the Gospel. In this sense, indeed, no one who believes the word of God can deny that Christ died for all men." Amyraut:* "The redemption purchased by Christ may be considered in two respects. 1. Absolutely, in relation to those who actually embrace it 2. Conditionally, as offered on such terms, that if any one will accept it, he shall become a partaker of it. In the former respect it is limited, in the latter universal. In like manner its destination is twofold: particular, as having the decree to bestow faith connected with it; universal, when it is considered separately from this decree." This writer says expressly,† "Since the misery of the human family is equal and universal, and the desire which God has to free them from it by a Redeemer, proceeds from the mercy which he exercises towards us as his creatures fallen into destruction, in which we are all equal; the grace of redemption, which he has procured for us and offers to us, should be equal and universal, provided we are equally disposed to its reception," &c.

Though all agree that Christ died for all men, yet they explain themselves differently in relation to the manner in which he died for all. As appears from the quotations given above, some say openly that

---

* Diss. de Gratia Universali.   † Tr. de Prœdest. cap. 7.

Christ died conditionally for all, and absolutely for the elect only. Others, perceiving that this view of the subject leads to gross absurdities, are unwilling to express themselves in this manner, and rather choose to say that Christ did not die for men on condition that they would believe, but that his death for all was absolute, whether they would believe or not. So that free access to salvation was opened for all who would by faith accept it; and, all obstacles being removed by the death of Christ, a way for a new covenant was opened equally to all men; all were placed precisely in the same salvable state. Yet they all come to this point, that Christ satisfied for all men severally and collectively, and obtained for them remission of sins and salvation; of which, if many are deprived, the cause is not to be sought in any insufficiency of Christ's death, nor any failure of will and intention on his part, but only in the unbelief of those who wickedly reject the salvation offered by Christ.

But the common opinion of the Reformed Church is, that Christ, from the mere good pleasure of his Father, was set apart and given as a Redeemer and Head, not to all men, but to a definite number, who by the decree of God constitute his mystical body. They maintain that for these alone, Christ, perfectly acquainted with the nature and extent of the work to which he was called, in order to accomplish the decree of their election and the counsel of his Father, was willing and determined to offer himself up a sacrifice, and to the price of his death added an efficacious and special intention to substitute himself in their room and acquire for them faith and salvation.

Whence we easily obtain a distinct statement of the question.

1. It does not respect the *value and sufficiency* of the death of Christ; whether as to its intrinsic worth it might be sufficient for the redemption of all men. It is confessed by all, that since its value is infinite, it would have been sufficient for the redemption of the entire human family, had it appeared good to God to extend it to the whole world. To this purpose a distinction is made by the Fathers and retained by many divines, "*that Christ died sufficiently for all, but efficiently for the elect only.*" This is perfectly true, if it be understood of the dignity of Christ's death, though the phrase is not accurate if it be referred to the will and purpose of Christ. The question which we discuss concerns the purpose of the Father in sending his Son, and the intention of the Son in dying. Did the Father destine his Son for a Saviour to all men and every man, and did the Son deliver himself up to death, with a design to substitute himself in the room of all men of all nations, to make satisfaction and acquire salvation for them? Or, did he resolve to give himself for the elect only, who were given him by the Father to be redeemed, and whose

Head he was to be? The pivot on which the controversy turns is, what was the purpose of the Father in sending his Son to die, and the object which Christ had in view in dying; not what is the value and efficacy of his death. Hence the question does not, as some learned divines have affirmed, respect the revealed will of God, but his secret will, his decree, to which, as all must agree, the mission and death of Christ are to be referred.

2. We do not inquire, respecting the *fruits and efficacy* of Christ's death, whether all will actually be partakers of these? which was anciently held by Puccius and Huberus. Our opponents extend these to believers only. But the question refers to the design of God in sending his Son into the world, and the purpose of Christ in his death. Were these such that Christ, by substituting himself in the room of each and every man, made satisfaction and obtained the pardon of sin and salvation for them all; or was his work designed for the elect only? Our opponents say the former; we say the latter.

3. We do not inquire whether the death of Christ gives occasion to the imparting of *some blessings even to reprobates*. Because it is in consequence of the death of Christ that the Gospel is preached to all nations, that the gross idolatry of many heathen nations has been abolished, that the daring impiety of men is greatly restrained by the word of God, that

multitudes of the human family obtain many and excellent blessings, though not saving gifts, of the Holy Spirit. It is unquestionable that all these flow from the death of Christ, for there would have been no place for them in the Church, unless Christ had died. The question is, whether the suretyship and satisfaction of Christ were, by the will of God and purpose of Christ, destined for every individual of Adam's posterity, as our opponents teach; or for the elect only, as we maintain.

We embrace this opinion for the following reasons:

I. The *mission and death of Christ are restricted to a limited number—to his people, his sheep, his friends, his Church, his body;* and nowhere extended to all men severally and collectively. Thus, Christ " is called Jesus, because he shall save *his people* from their sins."* He is called the Saviour of *his body.*† " The good shepherd who lays down his life *for the sheep,*"‡ and *"for his friends."*§ He is said " to die— that he might gather together in one, *the children of God* that were scattered abroad."‖ It is said that Christ " hath purchased *the Church* [or *his flock*] with his own blood."¶ If Christ died for every one of Adam's posterity, why should the Scriptures so often

---

* Matt. i. 21.   † Eph. v. 23.   ‡ John x. 15.
§ John xv. 13.   ‖ John xi. 52.
¶ Acts xx. 28.   Eph. v. 25, 26.

restrict the object of his death to a few? How could
it, with propriety, be said absolutely that Christ is
the Saviour of his people and of his body, if he is the
Saviour of others also? How could it in the same
way be said that he laid down his life for his sheep,
for the sons of God, and for the Church, if, according
to the will and purpose of God, he died for others
also? Would this be a greater proof of his love and a
firmer ground of consolation?

To this argument in general it is objected: (1.) "That
the Scripture, which in these passages appears to limit
the atonement to a few, elsewhere extends it to all."
This objection is more specious than solid. The universality alluded to is not absolute, but limited; one
which does not refer to all the individuals of the human family, but to individuals of all nations; as will
be shown at large hereafter. (2.) Another objection
is, " that in the texts quoted above, the satisfaction is
not considered separately, but in connection with its
application which is limited, though the satisfaction
separately considered is universal." To this we reply,
that the words and phrases which the Holy Spirit
uses in the texts cited above—such as, " *the Saviour*,"
" *to lay down life for one*," " *to give himself for one*,"
&c., properly denote satisfaction, the procuring of
salvation. And although they imply the application
of the thing obtained, yet this does not weaken the
force of the argument; because the atonement and its

application are inseparably connected, and are of the same extent; all which will be. proved in the proper place. (3.) Again, it is objected, that " Christ died absolutely for some and conditionally for others." This, however, takes for granted what ought to be proved. It is altogether gratuitous to say that Christ in his death had a twofold intention: one conditional, which extended to all; the other absolute, which was limited to a few. The Scripture nowhere countenances such a distinction; it always represents the *application* of the atonement as conditional, but the making of it never. The nature of the thing does not, indeed, admit of such a distinction; for, according to the hypothesis of the objectors, there was no consideration of the elect in the decree according to which Christ died; and they admit that he died with the same purpose with which the decree was passed; for the execution must be agreeable to the plan. Christ and the Father must have precisely the same object in view by his death. They say that the elect were separated by a posterior decree; but if Christ was destined to die for all before the elect were separated from the reprobate, he must have died for the elect and the reprobate in the same way. God decreed all things by one simple act, though we have to conceive of the decree by parts: who, then, can believe that in one simple act, God had two intentions so diverse, not to say contrary, that in one manner

Christ should die for all, and in another for some
only? Nay, since Christ could not will to die absolutely for the elect, without involving, by the law of
contraries, a will not to die for the reprobate, it is inconceivable how in one act he should will both to die
for the reprobate, and not to die for them. (4.) Another objection is, that " though these passages speak
of the elect, yet they do not speak of them exclu-
sively of all others; as, when Paul says that Christ
was delivered for him, he does not exclude others."
To this I answer, that though those texts upon which
I rely do not explicitly exclude all others, yet they
contain, in their description of those for whom Christ
died, certain circumstances which clearly exclude others. Though the blessing is promised to the seed of
Abraham, without saying to the seed of Abraham
alone, yet it is sufficiently clear that the blessing was
strictly confined to Abraham's seed. The object of
the passages quoted is to illustrate and magnify the
love of Christ towards his sheep for whom he lays
down his life; towards his Church and people for
whom he delivered himself up to death. But how
will this exalt the love of Christ towards them, if
they have no prerogative, no claims in his death
above the reprobate? Why should the immense love
of Christ, who lays down his life and sheds his blood,
be applied specially to the people of God? The example of Paul does not strengthen the objection; for

the apostle does not speak of this as a blessing peculiar to himself, but as one common to himself and the other elect or believers, to whom he proposes himself as an example, that they might be able to say the same thing of themselves because they were in the same state.

But there are also particular objections to each of the passages we have quoted.

To the words of the Evangelist Matthew, it is said, that "though Christ is called the Saviour of his *people*, in a peculiar sense, on account of salvation's being actually bestowed upon them, yet there is no reason why he should not be the Saviour of others also, on account of having obtained salvation for them, though, in consequence of their unbelief, they will never be made partakers of it; and that, in reference to this, Paul says that *God is the Saviour of all men, especially of them that believe.*"* It is gratuitous to say that Christ is the Saviour of some, for whom he has purchased salvation, but to whom it will never be applied. It is to take for granted what ought to be proved. The very expression, *to save*, denotes the actual communication of salvation. Christ is Jesus, not only because he is willing and able to save, and because he removes all obstacles out of the way of salvation, but because he does in reality save his peo-

* 1 Tim. iv. 10.

ple, both by meritoriously acquiring salvation for
them, and effectually applying it to them. That such
was the intention of God in sending Christ, and the
end of his mission, is clearly intimated by the imposition of the name Jesus by the angel. The passage
quoted from Paul's Epistle to Timothy does not show
the contrary; for the word which is in that passage
translated Saviour, in its most extensive sense denotes
Preserver; and when it is said that he is the Saviour
of men, the meaning is that he is the preserver of all
men, that he upholds or preserves them in their present
life. It is taken in a more strict and limited sense
when it is applied to believers, which is denoted by the
word *especially*. In what other sense than as the up-
holder of all men, can he be said to be the Saviour of
men who finally perish? To say that Christ, by his
death, intended to save them, will not solve the difficulty, for we do not call a man a saviour who *intends*
to save another, but him who does it actually. Now
Christ does actually uphold men in this life, for *in
him we live, and move, and have our being.** In this the
apostle alludes to a passage in the Psalms where God
is said *to save man and beast.*† Whence Chrysos-
tom, OEcumenius, Primasius, and Ambrose say " that
he is the Saviour of all in the present life, but of the
faithful only as to eternal life." And Thomas, " he is
the preserver of the present and future life, because he

* Acts xvii. 28.   † Psal. xxxvi. 7.

saves all men with a bodily salvation, and thus he is called the Saviour of all men; he also saves the righteous with both a bodily and spiritual salvation, and is hence said to be the Saviour *especially* of them that believe."

To the passage from John's Gospel, it is objected, " that those sheep, for whom Christ is said to have laid down his life, are not said to be the elect only." The context proves incontrovertibly that it can apply to none but the elect. Christ is speaking concerning sheep who hear his voice and follow him, whom he has known and loves intensely, and whom he must bring into one fold under one shepherd, (v. 15, 16.) Those sheep for whom Christ lays down his life, shall be put in possession of eternal life, and no man shall be able to pluck them out of the Father's hand, which things can be affirmed of none but the elect, who are called sheep, both on account of their eternal destination to life, and their actual and effectual calling in time. Nor let it be objected, " that he is said to have laid down his life for his sheep, because they alone shall enjoy the fruits of his death, whilst others, on account of their unbelief, receive no benefit from his expiatory sacrifice. Thus, to die for some, either signifies that death is suffered simply with an intention to profit some, which is true in respect of all; or, with an intention that they shall be profited in reality, which is true in relation to sheep only." For, in answer to this objection, consider that *to lay down life for some*, can no more be referred to the enjoyment of the fruits of Christ's death, than when it is said, that he gave himself a ransom for all.   There is no solid reason why the former phrase should be referred both to the intention and to the effect, but the latter restricted to the intention of bestowing help.   It cannot be conceived that there is any difference between these two.   He who dies for any one that he may profit him, intends that he for whom he dies shall be profited in reality; and he will in reality profit him if he can. Now, can any one assign a reason why Christ gains the object which he had in view, as to his sheep, but misses his aim as to the rest?   Equally unsubstantial is the objection, "that Christ could not lay down his life for his sheep as such; because, then they would have been his sheep before he died for them and purchased them for his own; hence, he died for them merely as sinners, which character belongs to them in common with others, and that hence he must have laid down his life in this way for others."   To this I reply, that though they were not actually his sheep, yet they were so by destination.   They had been given to Christ to be purchased and redeemed by him as the good shepherd who must shed his blood for their redemption.   By the decree of God they were given to him, before they were actually in his hands.*   Nay,

* John xvii. 24.

the mission of Christ is founded in that donation. "And this is the Father's will who hath sent me, that of all which he hath given me I should lose none, but should raise it up again at the last day."* Had there not been a fixed number contemplated by God when he appointed Christ to die, then the effects of Christ's death would have been uncertain, and the mystery of our redemption might have been rendered utterly vain and fruitless, by the perverseness of man in refusing to accept it.

To Ephes. v. 25, and Tit. ii. 14, the objection is, that "although Christ is said to have given himself *for his people, for his Church*, yet it is not expressly said that he gave himself for none others." We answer, that from the expressions used in these passages, and from the nature of the thing, it is clearly deducible that his offering of himself was so restricted. Because, the giving of himself, which the Apostle describes, arises from the love of Christ towards his Church as his spouse, and such a love necessarily excludes a similar love to others. In the preceding verse the Apostle gives this commandment, " *Husbands, love your wives.*" Now, though he does not add, " let your love of women be confined to your wives," yet all will acknowledge that such a restriction is necessarily implied in the Apostle's command. Who would hear, without indig-

* John vi. 39.

nation, the adulterer plead thus in vindication of his crime: "It is indeed said, *husbands, love your wives*, but it is not said, love those alone!" The giving of himself which is here attributed to Christ, is one which has for its object the sanctification of his Church and its salvation: both the procuring and applying of salvation, which belong to the elect and to the elect only. Since he delivered himself up for none except for this end, how can he be said to have delivered himself for those who will not attain that end?

It is objected to the passages Matt. xx. 28, xxvi. 28, and Heb. ix. 28, that " *many* is not opposed to all, but to one or a few, as is done Rom. v. 19, and Daniel xii. 1, and that *many* is often put for all." But the " many" of which the apostle and the evangelist treat, are described by such characters as cannot be applied to all men of all nations. For, of the many here spoken of, it is said, " *that he gave himself a ransom,*" or actually substituted himself in their room, that *he shed his blood for the remission of their sins*, and " *that he offered himself to bear their sins,*" i. e., that their sins might be through his atoning sacrifice really taken away. Though many is sometimes opposed to one or a few, yet it is not necessary, on that account, to understand it so in these passages, for it is often used when all cannot be included. Jerome, in his comment on Matthew xx., says, " The evangelist does not say that Christ gave himself for *all*, but for *many*, i. e., for all those who would believe," who are none other than the elect in whom God works both to will and to do. A gloss interlined on Jerome's book adds these words, " for many, not for all; but for those who were pre-destinated to life."

II. We further argue that the atonement was defi-nite, from the fact that Christ *was destined to die for none but those who were given him by the Father.* All men universally were not given to Christ, but a limited number only. Since, in the council of the Father which regulated Christ's death and defined its object, there was a designation, not only of Christ as Media-tor, but also of those for whose redemption and salva-tion he was to suffer; it is plain that he could die for those only who were in this sense given him. Here we may remark a twofold donation. One of Christ to men, another of men to Christ. Christ was given to men for the purpose of saving them, and men to Christ that through him they might be saved. The former is referred to in Isa. ix. 6, and xlix. 6, as well as in all those places in which he is said to be given and sent to us; the latter is alluded to in the places where mention is made of those given to Christ, as in John xvii. 2, 6, 12, and vi. 37. Seeing this twofold giving is reciprocal, each of them must be of the same extent; so that Christ is given for none but those who are given to him, and all those are given to Christ for whom he is given. Now, it is abundantly plain that some men only, and not all men, were given to Christ. This is asserted in many texts of Scripture, where those who are given to him are distinguished from other men. "Thou hast given him power over all flesh, that he might give eternal life to as many as thou hast given him. I have manifested thy name unto the men whom thou hast given me out of the world; thine they were, and thou gavest them me."* The Scripture designates those whom the Father gave him by such phrases as these: the people whom he foreknew;† heirs and children of promise;‡ the seed of Abraham, not carnal, but spiritual, both of the Jews and Gentiles;§ his people, his body, the Church;‖ vessels of mercy prepared to glory;¶ chosen in Christ, predestinated to the adoption of sons and to conformity to his image;** and the posterity of the second Adam, all of whom are to be quickened in Christ, in opposition to the posterity of the first Adam, in whom all die.†† From all which it appears, that Christ was not given for all of all nations, but for a limited number only.

To no purpose will our opponents reply, that "the giving of Christ was conditional, not absolute; that the condition was that all who would by faith receive

---

* John xvii. 2, 6.   † Rom. xi. 2.

‡ Rom. ix. 8.   § Rom. iv. 13. Gal. iii. 18. Heb. ii. 16.

‖ Matt. i. 21. Eph. v. 23.   ¶ Rom. ix. 24.

** Rom. viii. 30. Eph. i. 4, 5.   †† 1 Cor. xv. 22, 23.

the offered salvation, should be made partakers of it; and since this was not to be the case with all, it is not surprising that they derive no advantage from it." This is a begging of the question; it is without foundation in Scripture, which nowhere mentions such a conditional giving of Christ. Though faith is proposed as a means and condition necessary to the reception of Christ, and the enjoyment of the blessings offered in the Gospel, yet it does not follow that it was a condition to the giving of Christ, since faith itself is a gift of grace and one of the fruits of Christ's being delivered up for sinners. Further, if the giving of Christ rested upon any condition, the condition must depend either upon God or upon man. The latter of these can be affirmed by none but a Pelagian; if the former be affirmed, then it comes to this, that Christ is said to be given to us as a Saviour by God on these terms, that he will bestow him on us on condition of his working faith in us; which faith, however, he will not give, though he alone is able to give it. How glaring an absurdity!

Our view is further confirmed by the connection of that twofold relation to us, which Christ sustains: the relation of a Surety, and that of a Head. He is our surety, that he may acquire salvation for us, by rendering to justice that satisfaction which it demands. He is our head, in order to apply this salvation to us, by working in us faith and repentance, through the effectual operation of his Holy Spirit upon our hearts. Hence, as he is not given as a head to all men, but to his members only, or, which is the same thing, to the elect, who are actually to partake of salvation, he cannot be the surety or sponsor of any other than these. Of whomsoever he is the surety, he is also the head. The one cannot be extended farther than the other. This also appears from the connection between the death and resurrection of Christ, in which there is the same twofold relation. Since he died as surety, he must rise as head, as the reasons for his death and resurrection are the same; nor can any reason be given, why the ground of the one should be more extensive than that of the other. Hence it is, that the Apostle Paul speaks of these as being equal in efficacy and extent: "Christ died for our sins, and rose again for our justification"* "That he died for all, that they which live, should not live unto themselves, but unto him who died for them, and rose again."† Hence it cannot be said that he died for any others than those for whom he rose, because no one will be a partaker of the fruits of Christ's death, unless by his resurrection. But that he did not rise as a head to confer salvation upon all, is self-evident.

---

* Rom. iv. 25.   † 2 Cor. iv. 15.

III. The same doctrine is established by *the connection between the atonement and the intercession of Christ.* As they are both parts of his priestly office, they must be of the same extent; so that for all for whom he made satisfaction, he should also intercede, and not make atonement for those who will never have a place in his intercession. The object of his propitiation and of his appearance in the presence of God must be one, since the Apostles Paul and John represent their connection as indissoluble.* That he does not intercede for all, but only for those who are given him by the Father, Christ himself expressly declares: "*I pray not for the world, but for those whom thou hast given me out of the world.*"† When it is so much more easy to pray for any one than to lay down life for them, will any one say that Christ would die for those for whom he would not pray? Will they say that at the very moment before his death he would refuse his prayers on behalf of those for whom he is just about to shed his blood?

The objection which the Remonstrants or Arminians offer is frivolous: "that there is a twofold intercession of Christ: one universal, which is made for the whole world, of which intercession Isaiah speaks, liii. 12, and agreeably to which he is said to have prayed for his murderers;‡ another particular, which is made

* 1 John, ii. 1, 2. Rom. viii. 34.
† John xvii. 9.   ‡ Luke xxiii. 34.

for believers only, which is spoken of, John ix. and
Rom. viii." The objection rests not on any foundation, either in Scripture or reason. As Christ is always heard and answered by the Father,* if he prays
for all, all will be saved. The doctrine of universal
intercession is not taught by the Prophet Isaiah,
where he says, "*he made intercession for the transgressors;*"† for it is not said that he made intercession
for all, but for many whose character is delineated
by the prophet, in a preceding verse, as those who
shall be justified by Christ. It is not said, Luke
xxiii. 4, that he prayed for all those who crucified
him, but for those who knew not what they did; and
we are assured that these obtained pardon, no doubt
the fruit of the prayer which Christ offered up on the
cross to the Father.‡ Nor if Christ, through the im-
pulse of humane affections of love, prayed for those
who perished, is it to be considered that the intercessory prayers, which he offered as Mediator and in the
discharge of his special office, are to be extended to
others than the elect given him by the Father. To
the elect Christ himself restricts his intercessory
prayers.

This argument will not be weakened by objecting
that it is the world of unbelievers only, who are excluded from the prayers of Christ, those who are

---

* John xi. 42.   † Isa. xxiii. 12.   ‡ Acts ii. iii.

guilty of rejecting the Gospel, and hate believers, (v. 14,) but not the world chosen by God, for the redemption of which he has sent his Son.* The object of Christ's intercessory prayers is to obtain for believers perseverance in grace. The world, for which Christ says he does not pray, is opposed to those given him by his Father in the decree of election; the world, then, of which he speaks must embrace all the reprobate who were not given to Christ, and this antecedently to their rejection of the offered salvation. They were passed by as sinners, whether their sins were want of faith in the Gospel, or merely violations of the law of nature. As the act of God by which he chose to pass by a certain number of men and not appoint them to salvation, was done from eternity, there never existed a period when they, the world for whom Christ does not pray, were viewed in any other light, than as excluded from the benefits of his mediation and intercession. It forms no objection to this, that God is said "to have so loved the world, that he gave his only-begotten Son, that whosoever believeth on him should not perish;" because, as will be made to appear in the proper place, this does not extend to all men of all nations, but to the elect of every nation. Though he prays for the apostles who were then believers, and asks for them perseverance,

* John iii. 16.

6*

yet it does not follow that he prays for them as believers only, and in consequence of their faith: for
Christ (v. 19, 23) prays for all who should afterwards believe, " That they may be sanctified through
the truth and made perfect in one." Now, as this
sanctification and attainment to perfection could not
be effected without the instrumentality of faith, Christ
must have prayed for faith to be given them. Hence,
even that faith by which the Gospel is embraced, is
given to believers in consequence of Christ's intercessory prayers. Further, as Christ declares that he
sanctifies himself for those who are the objects of that
intercessory prayer, that they may be sanctified
through the truth; and as none are thus sanctified
but the elect, the conclusion is irresistible, that
Christ's intercessory prayers are extended to the
elect only, those who shall be saved with an everlasting salvation.

IV. The *inseparable connection between the gift of
Christ and the gift of the Holy Spirit* bears testimony
the most conclusive to the definite atonement. As
these two gifts, the most excellent which God has bestowed on us, are always in Scripture joined together
as cause and effect;* they must be of equal extent
and go together; so that the Son is not given

* John xvi. 7.   Gal. iv. 4, 6.   Rom. viii. 9.   1 John iii. 24.

to acquire salvation for any others. than those to whom the Spirit was given to apply the salvation procured. No reason can be assigned why the gift of the Son should be more extensive than the gift of the Holy Spirit. It is plain that the Holy Spirit is given to none but the elect. Hence, if there be any harmony between the work of the Son and that of the Holy Spirit, in the economy of salvation, Christ was given to die for the elect, and for them only. Pertinent to this purpose is the argument of the Apostle Paul, in which, from the giving of Christ, he infers the communication of every blessing. " He that spared not his own Son, but freely delivered him up for us all, how shall he not with him also freely give us all things?"* The apostle reasons from the greater to the less. Surely he who gave his Son, which incontrovertibly was the greater gift, will not refuse to give us faith and all other saving blessings, which are the less; and this the rather, because, as we shall presently prove, Christ, by delivering himself up, has merited for us, together with salvation, all those gifts. Whence the conclusion is inevitable: cither all those blessings shall be given to the reprobate, if Christ died for them; or if they are not given them, which is granted by all, then Christ did not die for them, i. e.; he did not die for all. This is not answered by alleg-

* Rom. viii. 32.

ing that the apostle speaks of Christ's being given in a special manner to the believers. For, as was said above, the supposition of a universal giving is gratuitous, and nowhere countenanced in Scripture; and since faith is a fruit of Christ's death, it cannot be a condition antecedent to his death. Further, since, according to the order which is laid down by our learned opponents themselves, the decree concerning Christ's death was antecedent to the decree relative to bestowing faith; it is inconceivable how at one and the same time, and in the self-same simple act, Christ could be delivered up for all, and for some only.

V. Another argument is, the *superlative love of Christ towards those for whom he died.* He loved them with the most ardent affection. Greater love has no one, than that one should lay down his life for his friend.* In the same exalted strain does the Apostle Paul extol the love of Christ:—he speaks of it as truly wonderful and unheard of among men. "Scarcely for a righteous man will one die, yet peradventure for a good man some would dare even to die. But God commendeth his love towards us, in that, while we were yet sinners, Christ died for us."† But this cannot be said of all men, and every man; for I presume that all men are agreed, that Christ

---

* John xv. 13.   † Rom. v. 7, 8.

loved Peter more than Judas. It is inconceivable how Christ could love with ineffable ardour of affection those whom, as an inexorable judge, he had already consigned, or had resolved by an irrevocable decree to consign, to mansions of endless woe and despair. It cannot with any colour of propriety be said that Christ and his apostle are treating of external acts of love. For, besides that external acts of love presuppose those which are internal; if Christ exercises to each and to all external acts of love so great that none can be greater, it follows that he has done, and still does so much for those who perish, that it is impossible for him to do more for the elect who shall be saved; than which nothing can be more absurd. Nor, if he loves some of the elect more than others, so far as regards the internal gifts of his Spirit, a diversity of which is necessary to the perfection of his mystical body, does it follow from this, that the disposition of his soul towards each of them as to the promotion of their good, is not supremely tender and affectionate.

VI. The same doctrine is inferred *from the nature of Christ's suretyship.* For it imports the substitution of Christ in our room, so that he died not only for our good, but in our place, as was said before, and proved against the disciples of Socinus. Hence, from the nature of his suretyship, he must assume to himself all the debt of those whose persons he sustains; and liquidate it as perfectly as if they themselves had done it in their own persons.   Can it be conceived that those for whom he died and satisfied in this manner, may yet be subjected to eternal vengeance, and bound to suffer again deserved punishment?   This question must be answered in the affirmative by all those who assert that Christ died for many who shall not be saved by his death; and yet to say so is to impeach the justice and veracity of God. For if, in consequence of his suretyship, the debt has been transferred to Christ and by him discharged, every one must see that it has been taken away from the primary debtors, so that payment cannot be demanded from them.   They must forever afterwards remain free, absolved from all obligation to punishment.   Pertinent to this purpose. are all those passages of Scripture which assert that our sins were so laid upon Christ, that the chastisement of our peace was upon him, and that by his stripes we are healed,* and those which declare that he was made a curse for us that we might be made the righteousness and blessing of God in him.†

VII. Christ died for *those only for whom he procured and to whom he applies salvation.*   As he procured and

---

* Isa. liii. 5, 6.   † 2 Cor. v. 21.   Gal. iii. 13.

applies salvation to the elect only, hence for them only he died. That Christ did not die for any but those for whom he procured salvation, and to whom he will apply it, appears, first, from the divinely appointed object of his death, which was to procure salvation for us; and, secondly, from the fact that the procuring cannot be separated from the application; what other end can there be in procuring a thing, but that it may be applied? A thing is procured in vain, which is never applied. Hence it follows, that if salvation is procured for all, it will and must be applied to all. If it be not applied to all, but to the elect only, then it was not procured for all, but for the elect only. In vain it is objected, " that Christ's death was not intended so much to procure salvation, as to remove all the obstacles which justice threw in the way to prevent God from thinking of our salvation." From this view of the subject, Christ rather procured for us the possibility of being saved than salvation itself, and placed it in the power of the Father to enter into a new covenant with man; an Arminian error long since condemned by the Synod of Dort as an injury to Christ's cross and to the efficacy of his mediation. How can Christ be said to have given himself a ransom, a price of redemption for us, to obtain for us eternal salvation, to redeem us from all iniquity, and other things of the same kind, which denote not the possibility, but actual procuring of salvation, if, after all, he only rendered it possible that we might be saved?

Another objection equally futile is, that " redemption was procured for all with a design that it should be applied to all, provided they would not reject it." This cannot be asserted with respect to an innumerable number, to whom Christ has never been offered, and who do not know him even in name. If it be alleged that Christ proposed to himself an object so vain and fruitless as a thing which was never to happen, and which could not happen without his gift, which he determined not to give, what an indignity is offered to his wisdom! It represents Christ as saying, I wish to obtain salvation for all, to the end that it may be applied to them, will they but believe; however, I am resolved not to reveal this redemption to all, and to refuse to innumerable multitudes to whom it is revealed, that condition which is the only means by which it can be applied to them. Shall men make the infinitely wise and holy Jesus say, I desire that to come to pass, which I know neither will nor can take place; and I am even unwilling that it should, for I refuse to communicate the only means by which it can ever be brought to pass, and the granting of this means depends upon myself alone? What a shameful indignity does this offer to the wisdom of Immanuel! It would be an insult to the understanding of frail man. Nor will the matter be amended by saying that the failure of the application is not to be attributed to Christ, but to the wickedness and unbelief of man. This is not less injurious to the honour of Christ, for it represents him either as not foreseeing, or as not capable of preventing those impediments, which obstruct the application of the salvation he obtained, and thus make it fruitless. They indeed allege that it was not in vain, though it fails of success; because, however men treat the salvation offered them, Christ will not miss the prime object which he had in view in his death; that is, to provide pardon and salvation for every man if he will only believe and repent—a thing which before was prevented by the inexorable rigour of divine justice. All this does not remove the absurdity. The object in procuring salvation could be none other than its application; and it cannot but be in vain, if it fails to accomplish this object. Christ needed to die for men, not to procure for them pardon and salvation under a condition which it is impossible for them to comply with, but to obtain for them actual pardon and redemption.

This is confirmed from the manner in which Christ procured salvation; for if the procuring extended to all, it must be either absolute or conditional. The former will not be asserted, for then all men, universally, would be saved. The latter is equally inadmissible; for, 1st. What is procured conditionally, is not, properly speaking, procured at all, but only a mere possibility of its being procured, provided the condition is complied with.   2d. Christ has procured the condition itself either for all, or for some only. If he has acquired the condition for all, then all will assuredly be saved; for this condition could be obtained for them in no other way than absolutely; unless, indeed, they would say that there is a condition of a condition, which is absurd, as tending to stretch out into an endless chain of conditions; yet even then all these conditional conditions will be, on the present supposition, purchased by Christ.   If the condition, by which the salvation is to be obtained, has been procured for some only, then the salvation has not been fully procured for all.   The procuring has been partial and defective in the most essential point.   In this view, vain and delusive has been the act by which salvation is said to have been provided; for the condition annexed to it is one with which the sinner is utterly unable to comply, which will never be performed, and which God not only foresaw would never be complied with, but also decreed not to give the power to fulfil, while he alone is able to give it.   Finally, this subterfuge represents Christ as having had a double intention in his atonement: one conditional, in favour of all; the other absolute, in favour of the elect; a representation unsupported by revelation, and irreconcilable with the unity and simplicity of the decree which appointed the death of Christ.

VIII. Another argument is found in the fact that Christ *did not purchase faith for all men.* Christ suffered death for those only, for whom he merited salvation, and with salvation all the means necessary to put them in possession of it, especially faith and repentance, and the Holy Spirit, the author of both; without which salvation is unattainable. That he purchased faith, repentance, and the graces of the Holy Spirit, for all men universally, cannot be said; for then all men would necessarily be saved by his death. He procured them for the elect only; therefore for the elect only he died. This argument is irresistible, unless it is denied that Christ purchased those means of salvation. But that Christ purchased faith for man, is proved by abundant scriptural testimony. 1. He is said to be* "the author and finisher of our faith." If he is the author of our faith, he must be its purchaser, for he bestows nothing on us, which he has not procured for us by his merits. 2. Christ is the meritorious cause of salvation. To him and his merits we are therefore indebted for every part of it, for everything which contributes to our salvation. But faith and spiritual life which he works and implants in us, are

* Heb. xii. 2.   Acts v. 31.

the chief part of our salvation. 3. Christ is the cause and foundation of all spiritual blessings:* "Who hath blessed us with all spiritual blessings in Christ." And of these faith is one of the greatest. Hence it is elsewhere said,† "It is given you on the part of Christ not only to believe on him, but also to suffer for his sake." In what other sense can faith be said to be given us for Christ's sake, but because he purchased it for us? 4. Christ promised to send the Spirit; who therefore is poured out or distributed by him. Hence the Spirit is spoken of as one of the fruits of Christ's death.‡ All the gifts of the Spirit, especially faith, are therefore the fruits of Christ's purchase. Here we are not to distinguish between the Spirit as sanctifying and comforting, and the Spirit as imparting spiritual illumination; as if Christ had merited the former only, and not the latter. For as all the graces of the heart proceed from the same Spirit, he who acquired for us the Spirit, the author of these graces, must also have acquired with him all his gifts; and as faith is the principle and root of our sanctification, he who purchased the Spirit who sanctifies, must also have purchased "faith, which purifieth the heart." 5. Christ could not be a full and perfect Saviour, unless he had procured for us faith, without which it is impossible to be made partakers of salvation. This doctrine

---

* Eph. i. 3.   † Phil. i. 29.   ‡ John xvi. 7.

has been uniformly taught in the Reformed Church. They maintained that Christ had not less procured for us faith, than salvation, and that he is the cause of all the gifts which the Father bestows upon us. Hence the venerable divines of the Synod of Dort, in their exhibition of the doctrines of truth, say,* " Christ, by his death, purchased for us faith and all the other saving graces of the Spirit." And to the same purpose, in their " Rejection of Errors,"† they condemn " those who teach that Christ, by his satisfaction, did not merit salvation for any definite number, and also that faith by which his satisfaction is efficaciously applied for salvation, but that he purchased no more than a power and entire willingness for the Father to enter into a new covenant with man, and to prescribe whatever conditions he might think fit; compliance with which conditions depended upon the free will of man; so that either all, or none might fulfil them. Such teachers think too meanly of the death of Christ, are ignorant of its glorious fruits and blessings, and recal from hell the Pelagian heresy."

It is a vain distinction which some make here respecting the decree. They say that " we must distinguish between the decree to deliver Christ up to death," and his death itself, which took place in time; that the decree to deliver Christ up to die for sinners

* Th. 8.   † Th. 3.

was antecedent to the election of a definite number, but his death procured the decree of special election." Amyraut,* speaking of Christ's death in time, says, "*Redemption ought to be equal, that it may respect all, as the creatures of God equally sinful,*" &c. He elsewhere says, that " the nature of the thing proves this, for seeing the affection of the Son must be the same with that of the Father for all men as his children; so the death of Christ in time, must be conformed to the eternal decree of the Father, as he would not make an atonement, unless according to the command of his Father. Therefore, since the decree of the Father respecting Christ's death proceeded from equal fatherly affection towards all, before any were elected to faith; Christ, in his death, could have no other end and intention than to execute his counsel." Even in this view of the subject, Christ, in his death, must have considered some as elect, and others as reprobate; for since there can be no election without reprobation, it was impossible for Christ to think of some as elected, without, at the same time, viewing others as passed by or reprobated. If, then, he willed to die for those whom he knew to have been elected, and that with a special affection for them as elected ones; he must, according to Amyraut, have been willing to die with the same

* De Prædesti. p. 77.

affection for those whom he knew to be reprobates, and that as reprobates; for Amyraut says, " he died to fulfil the decree of the Father, which proceeded from an equal love to all." Hence, this monstrous absurdity will follow, that Christ, out of the most ardent affection for those who he knew would never be saved, died with an intention and desire to save them; while both he and his Father had decreed that they should not be saved! It will not avail to free our opponents from this absurdity, to say, that he did not die for the reprobate formally as reprobate, but that he died for those as men, who at another time had been passed by, and thus excluded from salvation. Besides, that it is inconceivable how such abstractions can belong to a unique and simple decree; it would follow that Christ did not die for the elect as such. Here we reason by the rule of contraries. If Christ did not die for the reprobate as reprobate, we infer the same with respect to the elect. It appears inexplicable how Christ, in his death, could have respect to a first and a fourth decree, respecting the elect—that is, should have died for them, considered formally as elect, and materially as men; while as to the reprobate, he dealt abstractly, and viewed them only as men, and not as reprobate. For election and reprobation go hand in hand, and mutually imply each other.

But certain learned men, being aware that their hypothesis, which makes faith no fruit of Christ's death, but a gift of the Father, leads to great absurdities, offers indignity to Christ, and is injurious to salvation, have invented some other curious, intricate distinctions to escape these difficulties. Sometimes they teach, " that Christ did procure faith and repentance for all; conditionally, however." Again they say, "that he did not procure them in the way of satisfaction or meritoriously; but in the way of final cause, that faith might be given to the elect to bring them to Christ." But neither of these can be affirmed with truth. The former supposition is inadmissible; for how could faith be procured for us conditionally, when it is itself a condition? Although faith is usually represented as a condition, required to interest us in Christ; yet it is also held forth as one of the blessings of the new covenant, a blessing which Christ has purchased for us. Whence Christ is to be viewed as having procured for us not only salvation if we believe, but also faith that we may believe. The latter supposition is equally without foundation. In the schools of theology, no one ever before heard of a procuring, in the way of final cause, and not in the way of meritorious cause or satisfaction. The procuring of salvation and all things connected with it, is founded in the atonement and merits of the person who procures it. Then, if Christ did not procure for us faith in the way of meritorious cause, he did not merit faith. It cannot be said that Christ, in the way of final cause, procured faith for a limited number; for, on the hypothesis of those who make this distinction, there were none elected when God decreed that procurement, which Christ was to effect by his death. Again, either faith was procured in the way of final cause, for all those for whom salvation has been procured, or it was not. If the former be said, then, as they maintain that salvation has been procured for all, all will be saved. If the latter be said, then to what purpose has salvation been procured by the atonement for those who have not had procured for them, in the way of final cause, that faith, without which, they can never be made partakers of the salvation? Again, faith has been procured either for all in the way of final cause, or for the elect only. If for all, then all shall obtain it, which our opponents do not maintain. If for the elect only, then Christ, in and by his death, must have done more for the elect than for those who were not elected; while yet our opponents declare that, in passing the decree that Christ should die, which decree appointed and defined the objects of his death, God respected all men equally. Thus, in whatever light we examine this hypothesis, contradictions and absurdities grow out of it. Faith has been equally procured for all, but all will not be made partakers of it; or if it has not been procured for all, how vain and delusive is that procuring of salvation, which is

7

made only on the condition of faith, which he, who procured the salvation, knew it was morally impossible for the sinner to exercise, without special grace; and yet God, who alone can, has refused to give it! Hence, then, we arrive at this conclusion: either faith is completely in the power of the natural man, as Pelagius held, or it must have been procured by Christ in the atonement, and in consequence thereof given us by the Father.

To free themselves from all these difficulties, our adversaries sometimes attempt to illustrate their view of the subject, by a comparison instituted between Christ, and a prince who pays the price of redemption for all his subjects, who are taken captive by the enemy; though he does not effect by it the liberation of all; because some of them are unwilling to be set free. This comparison fails in one all-important circumstance. The prince is not able to give to those captives, who choose to remain in bondage, *the will* to avail themselves of the price of redemption, which has been paid. But Christ is able. Were there a prince, who could not only pay the ransom for his captive subjects, but could also give them the will to avail themselves of it; nay, further, suppose that the prince knew that they had not and could not have this will unless he bestowed it upon them, which he yet would not do; could any one say, that he really wished them to be liberated, and had paid the ransom with a serious intention to emancipate them? Again, if this comparison be urged, its force may be easily retorted. The corporeal liberation of a captive cannot be effected by the mere payment of a ransom; the chains and fetters which bind him in the prison must be broken asunder, otherwise the payment of the ransom will be ineffectual. In the same manner, in order to emancipate the soul from the spiritual bondage of sin, it is not enough that a ransom is paid to justice; the chains of sin and unbelief, which bind the prisoner so that he is both unable and unwilling to enjoy his liberty, must be burst asunder by the hand of the Almighty.

IX. Again, *if Christ died for all, then he made expiation for all their sins.* He therefore must have made atonement for the sins of unbelief and final impenitence, which prevent man from applying to himself the redemption provided for him; and thus they will no longer stand in the way of such an application; for on the supposition of satisfaction having been made for them, they must be pardoned. To this it cannot rationally be objected, that the blessing will be applied, if the condition on which redemption has been procured be complied with. It implies a contradiction to talk of the condition's being complied with, when the unbelief and impenitence are supposed to be final. It is as absurd to pretend that Christ died to atone for man's unbelief, provided he would not be unbelieving, but believe; as to say I have found out an infallible remedy for the healing of a blind or leprous man which shall be applied on this condition, that he will not be blind nor leprous. Further, a failure in fulfilling the condition cannot prevent the application of redemption to unbelievers; for it is supposed that Christ by his death has made satisfaction for unbelief, and thus has atoned for this very failure. But, since every one must see that this cannot be affirmed of those who will not be saved, or of the reprobate; the conclusion is irresistible, that Christ did not die for them.

X. The last argument on this subject is, *the absurdities that flow from the doctrine of universal atonement.* If Christ died for all men universally, it will follow:— 1. That he died, on condition they would believe, for multitudes innumerable, to whom his death has never been made known; and hence it was impossible that they could believe. 2. That he died for those whom he knew to be children of perdition, whom God had passed by, and who would never, to all eternity, enjoy any of the fruits of his death; and so exercised ineffable love towards those whom both he and the Father will cause to suffer eternally under the effects of their wrath. 3. That he died for those, who previously to his death were actually condemned without all hope of reprieve, and were in hell suffering his avenging wrath, and that as their surety he suffered punishment in the place of those who were suffering punishment for themselves, and must suffer it without end.   4. That Christ is the Saviour and Redeemer of those who not only never will be, but never can be saved or redeemed.   Or otherwise he must be an imperfect Saviour, having obtained a salvation which he never applies; for he indeed cannot be properly called a Saviour of any but those whom he makes to be partakers of salvation, and who are actually saved.

I proceed to answer objections.   Christ is nowhere in Scripture said to have died for all, unless some limitation is added; from which it may be inferred that these Scriptures do not teach that he suffered for all men of all nations, but that the object of his death is restricted according to circumstances.   Sometimes it is limited to the multitude of the elect, which has a universality peculiar to itself.   When it is said (2 Cor. v. 15) " *that Christ died for all*," it is not to be understood of all those " *who are dead*" in sin; for the object of the Apostle, in this chapter, is not to demonstrate the general depravity of men, but to show how great the obligations are which bind believers to the performance of duty, both on account of their justification through the imputation of the merits of Christ's death, which delivers them as fully as if they had made satisfaction in their own persons; and on account of their sanctification through the crucifixion of the old man

with his affections and lusts, by the efficacy of the
cross of Christ. Those are understood, who *live
not unto themselves*, but *unto Christ;* for whom Christ
not only died, but also *rose again;* and *whom the love of
Christ constraineth.* These phrases limit the *all* of the
Apostle. As if the Apostle had said, Christ died for
all who are described by these characteristics. They
agree to none but the elect, to whom alone it belongs
to die in Christ, and with him, as the Apostle elsewhere declares.* When the Apostle, in the 19th verse
of this chapter, says, " that God was in Christ reconciling the world to himself, not imputing their tres-
passes to them," he must be understood as treating of
the world of those actually reconciled, " to whom he
does not impute their sins." It is plain that this
agrees to none but to the elect. To all others he does
impute the sins which they commit. The Psalmist
says,† they are blessed to whom the Lord does not
impute sin. Surely this cannot be affirmed of those
who will never be saved. In the sense in which the
Psalmist speaks, and in which the Apostle speaks in
Rom. vi., we are to understand the words of the
Apostle, Rom. v. 18, 19: " By the righteousness of
one the free gift came upon all men to justification
of life; for as by one man's disobedience many were
made sinners ; so by the obedience of one shall many

* Rom. vi. 6, 8.   † Psal. xxxi. 1.

be made righteous." The *all men* who receive "justification of life," are those, " who receive abundance of
grace and of the gift of righteousness;" and they can
be none other than those who are actually justified.
Who are they that actually obtain justification? They
are believers, and believers alone; the elect, and the
elect alone, who belong to the body of Christ, which
is composed of all its members, and who are the *all* of
which the apostle speaks. As Adam is opposed to
Christ, Head to Head; as sin and death have passed
upon all who descend from Adam; in like manner, all
who pertain to Christ the second Adam obtain justification and life. The apostle. elsewhere expresses
this by the phrases dying, and being made, alive.*
" As in Adam all die;" that is, as all who die, die in
Adam, and on account of his sin; " so in Christ shall
all be made alive;" that is, all who will be "made alive"
in grace and glory, will be made alive in Christ and
on his account. All those for whom Christ is said†
to have " *tasted death*," are sons, who are either
brought or to be brought to glory, the captain of
whose salvation is Christ, whom Christ calls brethren,
and whom God has given him. Will any one say that
all these things can be affirmed of the reprobate?
When the objector is prepared to say so, then, and not
till then, let him quote this text, in proof of universal
atonement.

* 1 Cor. xv. 22. † Heb. ii. 9. Rom. x. 11.

Sometimes the sacred writers use the word *all* to exclude all distinctions of nation, age, sex, condition, character, and other particulars, by which men are distinguished from one another; and not with a view to comprehend every individual. Thus Paul says, " For the Scripture saith, whosoever believeth on him shall not be ashamed. For there is no difference between the Jew and Greek: for the same Lord over all is rich unto all that call upon him."* To the same effect he speaks elsewhere. " In him there is neither Jew nor Greek, circumcision nor uncircumcision, barbarian, Scythian, bond nor free: but Christ is all, and in all."† As if the apostle should say, no difference of nation or condition, either promotes or hinders salvation; but Christ is all, i. e., bestows all things necessary for salvation upon all who believe, without any regard to nation or condition. This is explained by John in the Apocalypse: " And they sung a new song, saying, Thou art worthy to take the book, and open the seals thereof: for thou wast slain, and hast redeemed us to God by thy blood, out of every kindred, and tongue, and people, and nation."‡ That is, from all the tribes of Israel, and from men of all nations, whether civilized or barbarous, hast thou redeemed us.

The passage so often in the mouths of our opponents,§ " Who gave himself a ransom for all, to be

* Heb. ii. 9.   Rom. x. 11.
† Col. iii. 11.   ‡ Rev. v. 9.   § 1 Tim. ii. 6.

testified in due time," teaches the doctrine which is illustrated in the foregoing section, and none other: 1. The *all* here spoken of, are those in whose place Christ substituted himself to bear their punishment and to pay the price of their redemption. This is the import of the word ἀντιλυτρον, as all the orthodox have maintained against Socinus and his disciples. This he cannot be said to have done for all; for then none could be condemned to suffer for his own sins. 2. Paul speaks of all those for whom Christ is Mediator by intercession as well as by satisfaction, for we have shown above that these two functions of his priestly office are inseparable. But the Arminians themselves admit that Christ does not intercede for all men. 3. The objects of the apostle's discourse are such as God " wills to be saved and to come to the knowledge of the truth." Experience teaches us that he does not so will with respect to all men universally. This we have proved at large under a former head, where the subject of God's desire to save all men is minutely examined. [We there remarked, that if God desires to save men who are not saved, his power must be limited, and who will dare say so? Besides, can we conceive that a being desires to accomplish an object and is unable to effect it, without also conceiving that being to be in some measure unhappy? At least we must suppose he would have been more happy had he gained his object; and who will dare to attribute imperfec-

7*

tion of happiness to God? Doubtless he who asserts that God earnestly desires the salvation of those whom he cannot save, must assert, that he is deficient both in power and happiness. Further, if there are men whom God desires to save and cannot, his not being able to effect their salvation must proceed from one of two causes: either the impossibility of making an atonement for their sins; or the obstinacy of their depravity is so great that he cannot vanquish it. The former of these cannot be said by our adversaries, for they assert that Christ made atonement for the sins of all men without any exception. The latter ground is untenable. From the great transgressors who have been made illustrious trophies of divine grace, we may and do safely conclude that the greatest and most obdurate sinners are equally, with the least guilty, in the power of grace. If sin be in some instances so potent as to be beyond the power of God to arrest and destroy it; who can say but that sin may so fortify itself in the dominions of God as to brave the utmost power of Jehovah's arm, and extend its ravages even to the throne of God? Hence the word *all*, used by the apostle in his letter to Timothy, must be understood in a restricted sense. That it is in some measure restricted must be admitted; for otherwise it would embrace fallen angels. How do we know that it does not extend to them? The Scripture assures us that he took not on him the nature of angels, and that there is no redemption for them. In the same way we learn from other portions of Scripture, which we have before adduced, that Christ did not die for all the posterity of Adam; without any exception.] The apostle is here to be understood as speaking of individuals of all nations, and not of all the individuals of every nation. Beza translates τους παντας, by a Latin word which signifies all kinds, some of all nations, states, and conditions. That this is the true sense of the phrase Calvin has proved by very solid reasoning. "The apostle simply means that no nation or order of men is excluded from the salvation, which God offers to all without exception who hear the Gospel." "The universality here mentioned must be referred to kinds of men, and not to persons; as if he had said, not to Jews only, but Gentiles also; not peasants only, but princes too, are redeemed by Christ."

The *world*, for which Christ is said by the Evangelist John* to have died, and to which he was sent, cannot be extended without limitation to the whole human family; for innumerable multitudes of the world which it composes, perish; but it denotes, either the universality of the elect, or some of all people indiscriminately, Jews and Gentiles. The evangelist alludes to the promise made to Abraham, that "in his seed [i. e., Christ] all families of the earth

---

* John iii. 16, 17, and iv. 42, and vi. 33.

should be blessed."* In this promise given to the ancient patriarch, there are blessings held out to all nations, who have Abraham for their father.† But this blessing belongs, not to all men universally, who are in the world, but to all the promised seed, without distinction of nation; as appears both from this, that all are not justified and saved by faith, which is the condition of the promise, as its blessing is explained by Paul;‡ and that the same apostle limits it to those who are the seed of Abraham *through faith*.§ Again, the apostle quotes this passage from Genesis, "In Isaac shall thy seed be called,"‖ and thus limits the promise to a definite number. Hence the world for whom Christ gave his flesh to death,¶ is none other than the world to which he is said (verse 33) to give life. "The bread of God is he which cometh down from heaven, and giveth life to the *world*," which cannot extend to the whole human family. For the giving of life imports its application and communication; which belong to the elect only. It is in this sense that Christ says he gives life to his sheep.** It is absurd to say that life is given to one when it is only obtained for him or offered to him, but never actually imparted. When Christ is said to be the "Lamb of God that taketh away the sin of

---

* Gen. xii. 3, and xxvi. 4, and xxii. 18.

† Rom. iv. 16.   ‡ Gal. iii. 8, 16.   § Rom. iv. 16.

‖ Rom. ix. 7.   ¶ John vi. 5.   ** John x. 28.

the world,"* the elect world is meant. The word
ἀίρεω, which is here translated " taketh away," signifies to remove entirely. How can Christ be said to
remove entirely the sins of the reprobate, which remain against them for condemnation? No other
world can be meant in these passages but the world
of the elect, made up out of Jews and Gentiles, without regard to nation or condition; the world of those
whose sins Christ is said to have borne in his own body
on the tree, that they, being dead to sin, might live unto
righteousness,† and who are said to be blessed, on
account of the taking away of their sins.‡

When it is said that " Christ is a propitiation for
our sins, and not for ours only, but for *the sins of* the
whole world," it is not meant to extend the propitiation to all collectively and severally, but to those only
who can comfort themselves by the intercession of
Christ, and the pardon which they have obtained
through him. They are the elect only. Christ is a
propitiation for those alone, whose cause he pleads as
intercessor with the Father; for these are joined together by the apostle as equal and inseparable. Our
learned opponents confess, in their explanation of
John xvii. 9, that Christ is not an advocate for all.
Besides, the Father must be actually propitiated and
reconciled to all those for whom Christ made propi-

---

* John i. 29.   † 1 Pet. ii. 24.   ‡ Psal. xxxii. 1.

tiation, unless we maintain that Christ missed his aim and shed his blood in vain, contrary to the apostle's assertion that no one for whom Christ died can be condemned,* which plainly cannot be said of those who are shut out from the covenant and have the wrath of God abiding upon them. Finally, the scope of the apostle, which is, to comfort believers against the remains of sin, proves that he does not intend every one of the posterity of Adam. For what comfort can a believer take from that grace which is common to the elect and the reprobate? What comfort if he knows that Christ in his death has done nothing more for him than for unbelievers? Therefore, the phrase of John has respect not to all men of all nations, but to the believing inhabitants of the whole world; or, as Calvin says, " the sons of God dispersed through the whole world." Lest any one should think that the blessing of Christ's atonement was confined to the apostles alone, or to those believers to whom this Epistle was directed; John says that it was much more extensive, embracing men of all nations, and belonging to believers redeemed out of every tribe, tongue, kindred, and people of the whole world. It is of little moment whether by the phrase *our sins*, are understood those of the apostles, or those of believing Jews of the dispersion, then

* Rom. viii. 34.

living, (to whom, without doubt, this Epistle was directed, as well as the Epistles of Peter and James, all which are called catholic, because not inscribed to any particular city or person,) as distinguished from those who either had believed before Christ appeared in the flesh, or who would afterwards believe to the end of the world. The question still comes to the same point. It is sufficient that the world here mentioned cannot embrace universally all men; as John and those to whom he writes were distinguished from it; while yet they are included in that universality, which embraces the whole of the human race. This was the opinion of Calvin. *"Not for our sins only* is added by way of amplification, that believers might be firmly persuaded that the propitiation extended to all who would embrace Christ by faith;" and again, "The object of John was none other than to make known that the blessing of which he discourses is common to the whole Church; therefore, under *all* he does not comprehend the reprobate, but designates them who would afterwards believe from among those who were scattered over every clime. Then truly with the greatest propriety the grace of Christ is illustrated, when he is preached as the only salvation of the world."

Though Christ came "to save that which was lost"*

* Matt. xviii. 11.

and saves none others, yet it is not necessary that he should save all those who are lost sinners. So far from this, Christ himself clearly testifies, that he came to call not those lost sinners who are both utterly ignorant of their lost state and swollen with an exalted opinion of their own righteousness, but those only who labour and are heavy laden with the burden of their sin.* Whence he says, he came to save that which was lost, in order to mark the *character* and *condition* of those who will be saved, but not *all* that which was lost. He designates the quality, not the number, of those whom he would save.

It is one thing to perish in reality and finally, another to receive from a brother an occasion by which he might, and, if left to himself, would perish. When the Apostle Paul speaks† concerning the perishing of a brother for whom Christ died, he does not intend actual perdition, as if one for whom Christ died might perish in reality, for none can snatch Christ's sheep out of his hand;‡ nor can any one of those perish whom the Father has given him to be redeemed;§ because they "are kept by the power of God through faith."‖ Especially since it is a *brother* who is here spoken of; he may be weak in faith, yet God is able to make him stand.¶ The apostle in-

* Matt. xi. 28.   † Rom. xiv. 15, and 1 Cor. viii. 10, 11.
‡ John x. 28.   § John xvii. 12.   ‖ 1 Pet. i. 5.
¶ Rom. xiv. 1, 4.

tends to develop the mischievous consequences of an improper and preposterous use of liberty in things which are in themselves indifferent, and show how it wounds and offends the conscience of a weak brother, and thus exposes him, as far as we can expose him, to the danger of perishing. The Scriptures often use words which naturally signify effects and actions, when nothing more is intended than to point out those occasions or motives which may lead to the effects and actions mentioned. Thus he is said to be guilty, as far as in his power, of adultery, who only looks upon the wife of another man to lust after her.* He is said to "*make God a liar*, who believes not the record which God has given of his Son."† That is, he does it, so far as in him lies. No one will say that he does so in reality. In this way a weak brother is said to perish by our knowledge, when we do nothing to preserve him; as it is expressed Rom. xiv. 15: "Destroy him not by thy meat."

When heretical, apostate teachers are said "to deny the Lord that bought them,"‡ we are not to understand the buying to mean a literal atonement redeeming the sinner from the wrath and curse of God, and from eternal death. No one is so redeemed, but those who were given by the Father to Christ to be redeemed, and who consequently will be kept by

---

* Matt. v. 28.　　　　† 1 John v. 10.　　　　‡ 2 Pet. ii. 1.

Christ and saved with an everlasting salvation, as
the members of his body and his peculiar treasure.
It is deliverance from error and idolatry of which
Peter here speaks; a deliverance effected by an out-
ward exhibition of the Gospel, and a setting apart to
the ministry, for which these false teachers were in a
certain respect bought by Christ as Lord of the
Church. Christ had acquired a peculiar title to
them, as his own, by calling them into his Church,
the house which he owns, as masters formerly bought
servants for the discharge of domestic duties. That
this is the intention of Peter is collected from the following considerations:—1. He uses the word δεσποτης,
which signifies a master or an owner rather than a
Saviour, to whom redemption properly so called belongs. 2. The word αγοράζειν which the apostle here
employs is generally used to express that kind of buying which is practised in markets, and often denotes
simple deliverance. 3. The kind of buying here contemplated, is that through which those bought are
said " to have escaped the corruptions that are in the
world, through the knowledge of God our Saviour,"
by which " they have known the way of righteousness." All these belong to deliverance from pagan
errors and idolatries, and to a calling to the knowledge of the truth, from which, through apostacy and
the introduction of most pernicious heresies, they make
defection. Hence they are said to deny their Master

who bought them and called them to the work of the ministry. [4. The denying of the Lord here mentioned, is a sin which is spoken of as peculiarly aggravated; and that which constitutes the peculiar aggravation is, that they deny their Master who bought them. But if Peter intends by the purchase here mentioned, that atonement which Christ in his death made for sin, then there was nothing in the conduct of these teachers peculiarly wicked; the same thing might be affirmed of every man, upon the hypothesis of our opponents; for they maintain that he bought every man. On the supposition, however, that the buying here intended is the calling of these false teachers out of the darkness of heathen superstitions, to a knowledge of the glorious Gospel of God, and making them teachers of that Gospel; then their denial of a Master who had done such great things for them, was a crime aggravated by the foulest ingratitude.—*Trans.*]

Sanctification by the blood of the covenant may be understood in a twofold sense. One internal, spiritual and real, which belongs to those who are actually redeemed and regenerated by the blood of Christ; another external and apparent only, which consists in a profession of the truth. The former necessarily presupposes that Christ died for those who are thus sanctified. The latter kind of sanctification does not presuppose this at all. Many hypocrites obtain that external sanctification, by an external calling to mem-

bership in the Church, and the enjoyment of its privi-
leges, especially baptism and the Lord's Supper; to
whom, notwithstanding, Christ with his saving benefits does not belong; because they are destitute of justifying faith. When Paul speaks of those who pro-
fane the blood of the covenant wherewith they had
been sanctified,* we cannot suppose (upon the hypothesis of the Reformed churches) that he intends the internal and real sanctification of which we have spoken.
We must understand him to mean external sanctification, such as belongs to those who profess their adherence to the Church and enjoy its ordinances, especially
baptism, in which they are sanctified or set apart from
the world by the sprinkling of water which represents
the blood of the covenant, and who renounce it by
denying Christ and apostatizing from his Gospel. In
this manner, those who eat and drink unworthily, at
the sacrament of the Supper, are said to be guilty of
the body and blood of Christ.† Besides, the apostle
speaks hypothetically, not absolutely. He points
out the connection between an antecedent and consequent. He shows what they who thus transgress are
to expect. He asserts nothing more respecting those
who are really redeemed and true believers, than what
is elsewhere asserted respecting himself and angels
from heaven.‡ "Though we or an angel from

* Heb. x. 29.   † 1 Cor. xi. 27, 29.   ‡ Gal. i. 8.

heaven preach any other doctrine, let him be accursed." But no one will infer from this, that the apostle or an angel from heaven will be accursed.

What every one is bound to believe absolutely and simply, directly and immediately, without anything previously supposed, we grant is true. But the case is different in relation to those things which one is bound to believe mediately, and in consequence of some acts supposed to be previously done. It is false, however, that all men are bound to believe that Christ died for them simply and absolutely. In the first place, those to whom the Gospel has never been preached, to whom Christ has never been made known, are not surely bound to believe that Christ died for them. This can be affirmed of those only who are called in the Gospel. "How can they believe in him of whom they have not heard, and how can they hear without a preacher?"* Secondly, even all those who hear the Gospel are not bound to believe directly and immediately, that Christ died for them, but mediately. The acts of faith and repentance are presupposed; they must precede a belief that Christ died for one's self; for Christ's death belongs to those only who believe and repent. So far is it from being true that unbelievers are bound to believe that Christ died for them, that he who persuades them so to believe mis-

---

* Rom. x. 14.

erably mocks them; since the wrath of God abides on
them, and they are bound to believe themselves condemned already.* Nor, if they are bound to believe
that Christ has died for them, provided they repent
and fly to him, does it follow that this is simply and absolutely true whether they believe or not. Hence those
who are bound to believe that Christ died for them,
are not simply and absolutely all men; it is all those
only who are weary and heavy laden with their sins;†
who thirst and sensibly feel their need of drink;‡ or
who are penitent and feel their misery.

It will not avail here to object, that "faith in Christ
is demanded of all who hear the Gospel, and that not
an undefined faith, but a faith true and justifying,
which it cannot be unless it terminates on Christ as dying for them." For, although faith in Christ is so demanded, and that a true and justifying faith, yet we
may not infer that it is required that all its acts are
immediately and at the same time to be exercised;
and especially its ultimate and special act, that of believing in Christ as having died for me. For, although this is included in the acts of justifying faith,
yet it is not its first act which is immediately and in
the first instance demanded of the person called in
the Gospel; it is its last, and presupposes others preceding it. That this remark may be well understood,

* John iii. 36.   † Matt. xi. 28.   ‡ Isa. lxi. 1.

I shall proceed to distinguish various acts of faith. First, one act of faith is *direct*, which has for its object the offer of the Gospel. By this act I fly to Christ and embrace his promises. Another act is *reflex*, and has for its object the direct act of faith. By this act I discover that I have indeed believed, and that the promises of the Gospel belong to me. Again, the direct act of faith is twofold. One of its operations consists in the *assent* which it gives to the word of God and the promises of the Gospel, as true in relation to the giving of salvation to all who repent and by a living faith fly to Christ and embrace him. Another operation of saving faith is its *taking refuge* and *trusting* in Christ, acknowledging him as the only sufficient Saviour. It is by this we fly to him, rest in him, and from him obtain pardon of our sins and salvation. Now, that faith which is commanded in the Gospel is commanded as to the first and second acts which are direct, before it is commanded as to the third act which is the reflex, and which necessarily supposes the two former; as it cannot exist unless preceded by them. Hence we are enabled clearly to detect the fallacy of the above objection. When the objection speaks of the faith commanded, it refers to that act by which the sinner lays hold of Christ; but when it speaks of the thing believed, then it refers to the last, by which we believe from the evidence furnished by the direct act in our souls, that Christ died for us. Christ is not

revealed in the Gospel as having died for me in particular; but only as having died in general for those who
believe and repent.   Hence I reason from that faith
and repentance which I find actually to exist in my
heart, that Christ has, indeed, died for me in particular.   I know that he died for all who fly to him; I
find that I have fled to him; hence I can and should
infer that he died for me.   That the faith commanded
in the Gospel is not a direct and immediate belief that
Christ died for me, appears from this consideration:
that when it is enjoined either by Christ or his apostles, no mention is made of its being applied to this or
that man, in particular.   It is set forth only in a general relation to duty, or to blessings promised to those
who believe; as in Matt. xvi. 16.   Peter, in his celebrated declaration of faith, professes no more than
this: *that he believes Jesus to be the Christ, the Son of
the living God.*   John vi. 69: " We believe and are
sure, that thou art that Christ, the Son of the living
God."   Paul demands no more of those who believe
unto salvation, than " to confess with the mouth the
Lord Jesus, and to believe with the heart that God
raised him from the dead."*   Thus, when the saints are
commanded to believe in the Son of God, they are
bound indeed to believe that Christ is the true Messiah, and to fly to him as the only author of salvation,

---

* Rom. x. 9.

to those who, through faith and repentance, betake themselves to him; and these acts must take place before they are bound to believe that Christ died for them.

Hence it appears, that the command to believe in Christ, embraces many things before we come to the last consolatory act, by which we believe that he died for us. First, we are to believe what the Scripture reveals to us, relative to our miserable condition by nature and our utter inability to effect our own salvation. Whence arises a salutary despair of our own exertions, and a knowledge of the necessity of a remedy. Secondly, those who thus despair of themselves, are commanded to believe that Christ, the Son of God, is the alone all-sufficient Saviour, given by God to men— that in him alone, they can obtain perfect salvation and remission of sin, who sincerely fly to him and repent with genuine repentance. Thirdly, those who are thus contrite and penitent and despairing in themselves, are commanded to fly to Christ as the rock of salvation; to embrace his merit as all-sufficient; to fall upon and sweetly rest upon it; and through it alone to expect remission of sin, righteousness and salvation. Fourthly and finally, those who perceive that they do repent, fly to Christ, and repose in him all their hopes of salvation, are bound to believe that Christ died for them, and that on account of his death their sins are pardoned. From all which, it is abun-

8

dantly plain, that faith in Christ presupposes an afflicting sense of misery and a desire of deliverance; and that the command to believe does not respect all indiscriminately, but only all who feel their misery and desire deliverance from it, who hunger and thirst, who labour and are heavy laden, who are broken in spirit and contrite in heart.* Further, it appears that this Gospel command does not immediately and in the first instance, demand of us that act of faith, by which we believe that Christ died for us, but that by which we fly to Christ, embrace him, and rest on him, which is nothing else than the one by which the penitent sinner, dejected under a sense of his misery and awakened by the call of the Gospel, renouncing every other hope, flies to Christ as the rock of salvation, and with his whole heart desires and seeks the grace offered in the Gospel. To express it in a word, the faith which the Gospel demands of those who hear it is, *the flying of the sinner for refuge to God as the fountain of grace, and to Christ as the ark of safety which is opened in the Gospel.* If I am conscious to myself that I have done this, which is the formal act of faith, then I can and ought to exercise the other act by which I believe, that for me, who repent and fly to him, Christ hath died. This is sometimes called the *consequent* act of faith, because it follows the direct act of faith, by

* Matt. xi. 28, and Isai. lxi. 1.

which I believe in Christ and fly to him as the only and perfect Saviour. It is also called the *consolatory* act, because it pours into the soul of the believer unspeakable joy and consolation. Since, therefore, no one can have this special reflex act of faith, unless the other acts together with repentance are presupposed as going before it; we infer, that all are not bound to believe that Christ died for them, but only believers and penitents, or all who, through the knowledge of sin and a sense of the divine wrath, are contrite in heart, and fly to him, and from him seek pardon of sin, and rely on his merits alone for salvation.

In vain will any one reply, (1.) " That the command to believe in Christ calls for a faith embracing all its acts, and among them the last, by which we believe that Christ died for us, and that this is required of all who hear the command to believe." The nature and dependence of these acts upon one another is such, that the last cannot exist without both the former; the third cannot exist without the second, nor the second without the first. When, therefore, the command to believe is announced, the first act is demanded of the sinner; not that he may halt there, but that, having performed it, he may go on to the second. But in case he has not performed the first, he is by no means required to go on to the second. He cannot, nay he ought not to believe, that Christ is his Redeemer, who does not believe that Christ is the Son of God and the

Redeemer of men; nor should a man believe that Christ redeems him, while yet he does not believe that Christ is a Redeemer at all. But, when a man finds in himself the preceding acts, which are the foundation of the last, then, and not till then, let him go on to exercise that last one also.

Equally vain is the objection, (2.) "That as many as are commanded to believe in Christ, are commanded to have justifying faith, as no other can be saving; but justifying faith necessarily imports that we believe not only that Christ died in common for men, but for us in particular; that otherwise, this faith would not differ from the mere historical faith of reprobates; nay, it would not differ from the faith of devils, who can believe the same thing." To this I reply, that the justifying faith which is commanded in the Gospel, does indeed embrace the various acts of which we have spoken, but every one in its own order. First, the direct and formal act, which consists in the last judgment of the intellect, (or that by which the will is immediately impelled to volition,) concerning Christ, that he is the sole and perfect Redeemer of all those who believe, repent, and seriously fly to him. This is called justifying faith. In it the light let into the understanding powerfully impels the will, and the whole soul flies for refuge to Christ and finds rest. Secondly, the reflex and consolatory act, which follows of itself, when the first is performed. From the time that I feel myself powerfully persuaded by the Gospel call and promises, seriously to fly to Christ, and expect life and righteousness from him alone, from that moment I can and should infer, that Christ has died for me; because, from the Gospel I learn, that he has died for all who believe and repent. Hence the answer is easy to the argument: Whosoever is bound to have justifying faith, is bound to believe that Christ died for him. I deny that this is true of the first act of faith. Of the second reflex act, I admit it to be true. Presuppose the first, then we are bound to believe that Christ died for us; exclude it, then I deny that any man is so bound. Nor is, therefore, the faith of believers like that of reprobates and devils. For, although reprobates may believe theoretically that Christ is the Son of God and Saviour of men, yet they are never so truly persuaded by a fiducial assent to the word of God, that they fly to him and rest upon him for salvation. If they were truly persuaded that Christ is the only and perfect Saviour of all who believe and repent, and that out of him there is no salvation, it would be impossible for them not to fly to him and embrace him for salvation with their whole heart. This necessity arises from the will's always obeying the last dictate of the understanding, and from all creatures seeking their own happiness. Hence also it appears, that the faith of devils has nothing in

common with that of the elect. For the devils know
that Christ is offered to men alone, and that they
have no interest in him; and it is impossible for them
to place any fiducial reliance upon him.

Again, it is objected, (3.) "That no one can place
his trust and reliance upon Christ, unless he knows
that Christ has died for him and is his Saviour. For
man always is anxious about his salvation, until he
knows the intention of God and the will of Christ,
and that by the purpose of God the death of Christ
was destined for him." To this I reply, that there
are two acts or parts in the fiducial reliance of the
Christian. The one consists in his receiving and
taking•refuge in Christ; the other, in the rest and
consolation which arise from a sense of having fled to
and received Christ. The former is the act of faith,
by which we fly to Christ as the only Saviour, cleave
to him, and appropriate him to ourselves for salvation. The latter is the act by which, flying to Christ
and resting on him, we trust that we have, and to
eternity will have, communion with him in his death
and its benefits; and joyfully repose in the firm per-
suasion that he died for us, and by his death reconciled us to God. Some divines call the former *faith
on Christ*, and the latter *faith respecting Christ*. This
respects Christ as having died for us; not so the
former; for no one can know that Christ has died for
him, unless he has first believed on him. As Christ

is promised to those only who believe and repent, I must first fly to him and embrace his merits with genuine repentance, before I can on good grounds decide that the death of Christ belongs to me by the decree of God and the intention of Christ. My faith, however, does not cause that Christ died for me; for his death was antecedent to any regard had to faith as its meritorious cause, and the grace of faith is a fruit and effect of the death of Christ. But it is an evidence in all those who possess it, that Christ died for them. We infer the existence of the cause from the effect. And though I cannot yet assure myself that Christ has died for me, it does not follow that I must always remain in a state of doubt and anxiety, and that my faith must be weak and unstable. My faith may firmly rest upon the general promises of the Gospel to every believing and penitent sinner. Hence by certain consequence, when I find that I possess faith and repentance, I may assure myself that these promises belong to me.

Another objection is, (4.) " That, by our hypothesis, the foundation of the sinner's consolation is taken away, as we reason from a particular to a universal; thus, Christ died for some; therefore, he died for me. But by the rules of good reasoning, we should proceed from a universal to a particular; Christ died for each and every man; therefore, he died for me." But it is gratuitous to say that we reason in this way, which

every one sees to be absurd.   On the contrary, we
reason from a universal to a particular, but in a certain order.   Christ died for all who believe and repent;
but I believe and repent; therefore, he died for me.
Besides, it is false that any ground of consolation
can be drawn from the absolute universality of Christ's
death; for that which is common to the godly and
ungodly, to those who shall be saved and the multitudes who have been or shall be damned, can surely
afford no solid comfort to any one.   If it be supposed
that Christ died for Judas and Pharaoh, who have
perished notwithstanding, how can this free me from
the fear of damnation?   If you reply, that this fear
may be taken away by faith, you admit that the atonement is not for all men, but for all believers.   Your
argument is: Christ died for all who believe; but I
believe; therefore he died for me, and I shall be saved;
" for whosoever believeth on the Son shall not perish,
but have everlasting life."   This is exactly our mode
of reasoning.   Further, no solid peace can be extracted from that which is insufficient for salvation, which
avails not, and of itself cannot avail, to prevent damnation.   And such is that universal grace for which
our opponents contend, a grace which is never effectually applied to the sinner.   What will it avail the
sinner to know that Christ died for all, while it is certain that, without faith, no one will ever become a
partaker of the fruits of his death?   Since faith is not

given to all, will he not be always anxious to know
whether he belongs to the number of those to whom it
will be given?   May not the same difficulties and scruples which can be urged against special grace and a
special atonement, be also urged against a special
decree of bestowing faith?   If it be necessary to solid
peace of conscience to hold that the mercy of the
Father is to all and the redemption of the Son for all,
it is equally necessary to hold that all are actually
called and all experience the grace of the Spirit.   If
the sinner anxiously say, who knows whether Christ,
since he has not died for all, had died for me? may he
not also say, who knows whether God will give me
faith, and whether I am of the number of the elect or
of the reprobate?   Besides, all such scruples originate
from a desire to know what it is not given to man to
know, at least, not in the way in which these people
seek to know it.   It becomes no mortal to institute a
scrutiny, *à priori*, into the secrets of the divine decree,
relative to election and reprobation.   In such inqui-
ries a man should proceed *à posteriori*, by examining
himself, in order to discover whether he has truly
repented of his sins or not.   If he has, he may, and
ought to assure himself of the grace of God and his
own election.   If he has not, he ought, without delay,
to apply himself to the use of the means which God
has appointed; he ought to hear, and read and ponder
the Word, and pour out ardent prayers to God for the

gift of faith and repentance. Nor can any scruples occur on this subject, which our learned opponents are not as much bound to remove as we; unless, with the Arminians, they maintain that every man has of himself, through the universal grace of God, sufficient power to believe and repent. But those against whom we have reasoned in this chapter, have, through the grace of God, always thus far professed to reject this dogma, as evidently Pelagian. The foundation of consolation, therefore, is to be sought, not from the universality of the atonement, but from the universality of the promises to all who believe and repent.

Although the reprobates who do not believe the Gospel will be deservedly condemned for their unbelief, yet it does not follow that they were commanded to believe that Christ died for them. There are various kinds of unbelief besides that of not believing that the atonement was made for them: such as, not believing that Jesus is the Son of God, and the Messiah sent by God, but that he was a false prophet and an impostor; or the not believing that faith in him is a condition necessary to salvation. All these are acts of unbelief, and that of a very criminal nature, though those who are guilty of them may never have thought of Christ's dying for them. That faith which Christ so often demands, and for the want of which he so severely reprehends the Jews, embraces in itself many things which must have preceded their belief thát Christ is their Saviour and Redeemer. This, indeed, is not a thing which the Jew was immediately to believe. He must first have believed that salvation is not to be obtained by the law, either in its ceremonies or legal works; that it is to be sought only in the Messiah promised in the prophets; that Jesus of Nazareth is that Messiah; and that all will be saved who believe in him. All these general acts of faith must have preceded the belief that Christ had died for him. Nor can it be replied, that all these acts, and, above all, the special, appropriating act, are comprehended in the command to believe on Christ. As we have said above, though all these are commanded, yet it is in a certain order, and the latter are not commanded in any other way than as preceded by the former; and, on the supposition of the first acts not having been performed, it is impossible that the latter should be.

Though God, by the preaching of the Gospel, offers Christ to sinners, it does not follow that he must have died for all those to whom he is thus offered, or else the offer cannot be sincere. Because the offer is not absolute and simple, but it is made under the condition of faith and repentance. It is true, not in the way of an accurate historical statement, which, whether believed or not, always remains true; but in the way of promise, the truth of which is ascertained when its condition is complied with, as Camerus de-

clared. It does not say to the sinner, Christ has
died for you, and you shall be saved on account of
this death, whether you believe or not. But it in-
forms him that salvation is procured by the death of
Christ; that it is for all who believe; and that, by
embracing it in faith, the sinner will find this to be a
consolatory truth. From which it follows, that there
is an indissoluble connection between faith and salvation; and that all who wish to enjoy Christ and
his benefits, and who are called by the Gospel, are
bound to exercise faith. But from this Gospel call,
we by no means rightly infer that God, by his eternal
and immutable decree, has destined Christ to be the
Saviour of all who are called, or that he intended
that Christ, by his death, should acquire salvation for
each and every man. For the Gospel which is
preached to those who are called, does not declare
that, in the eternal decree of God, it has been ordained that in Christ redemption has been procured
for each and every man. It rather announces to sinners a divine command, with a promise annexed, and
teaches what is the duty of those who wish to be
made partakers of salvation. We must not suppose
hence, that such an offer as this is adverse to the
divine decree. Because, though it does not answer
to the decree of election, yet it answers to the decree respecting the means of saving those who are
elected. In the decree (*de personis*) of election, God

ordained Christ as the Saviour of the elect, and his death as the price of their redemption; and determined to bestow upon them that faith which should enable them to embrace the salvation procured by this death. Of this decree, the internal, saving operations of the Spirit are the expression and execution. In the decree (*de rebus*) respecting the means of salvation, God was pleased to connect Christ and faith together, and to offer Christ to the hearers of the Gospel. The preaching of the Gospel corresponds with, and is the execution of, this decree. It is of this decree that Christ speaks, when he says, "And this is the will of him that sent me, that every one who seeth the Son and believeth on him, may have everlasting life."* Promises thus conditional, made to those who believe and repent, unfold the connection which God has established between faith and salvation; and make known that those hearers only of the Gospel shall be saved who believe and repent. They, however, no more show that Christ died for all the hearers of the Gospel, than that they shall all believe and obtain pardon of sin. From the remission which they obtain who believe and repent, it is proved that Christ died for them; and it would also be true, if others believed and repented, that Christ had died for them. But he who argues from this

* John vi. 40.

that Christ has died for all, on the condition that they would believe, reasons falsely; for, from hypothetical premises, he draws an absolute conclusion, contrary to all good rules of reasoning.

Here let me crown this chapter by adding the judgment of Deodatus and Tronchin, the celebrated theologians deputed to the Synod of Dort, who, in the name of the whole Genevan Church, presented this to the venerable Synod, as the common faith of the Church, never to be given up. *De Univers. Gratiæ, Cap. II.* " Christ, out of the mere good pleasure of his Father, was appointed and given to be the Mediator and Head of a certain number, who, by the election of God, were constituted his mystical body."—(Th. 1.) " For these, Christ, fully aware of the divine purpose, willed and decreed to die, and to add to the infinite merit of his death a special intention to render it efficacious."—(Th. 2.) " The universal propositions which are found in Scripture, do not mean that Christ, according to his Father's purpose and his own intention, died and made satisfaction for all and singular of the race. But they are to be restricted to the totality of Christ's body; or else to be referred to that feature of the new Covenant, by which the Son receives for his inheritance all nations, without regard to external distinctions; that

is, at his pleasure sends the ministry of the Word to
all tribes and races indiscriminately, and out of them
gathers his Church.   This is the foundation of the
general call of the Gospel."—(Th. 6.)

BOOKS IN THE TWINBROOK SERIES